Paul Benjamin

When Geese Fly South!

By Paul Benjamin

The American Church Growth Study Series:

The Growing Congregation

The Growing Congregation
Study Guide

How in the World?

How in the World?
Study Guide

The Equipping Ministry

The Equipping Ministry
Study Guide

The Vision Splendid Series:

Book One: Believing

Book Two: Being

Book Three: Thinking

Book Four: Working

Book Five: Relating

Book Six: Resting

Maxims Series:

Maxims I

Maxims II

Christian Growth

KUDOS

This book should be an encouragement to all those who are facing hard times.

DOLAN L. BAKER

WHEN GEESE FLY SOUTH! is a story that needs to be told.

ERNEST H. CHAMBERLAIN

. . . has been a great source of encouragement and hope for me. P.S. I love the excellent quotes.

TOM CLARK

Those who feel that their influence and ministry are in peril will appreciate this book: those who need encouragement to persevere a little longer will find it here.

PAT L. HARTSON

To those of you who labor in hostile climates, before you throw in the towel in the leadership ministry, read this book!

KEN IDLEMAN

This book can serve as an encouragement to all who minister by helping them deal honestly with their setbacks, rather than keeping them secret in order to sustain a perception of success.

BRYCE JESSUP

Who would ever guess that one of the world's most dangerous mission fields is in the Washington, D.C., metropolitan area? It's ironic that the Wilderness has turned up again in America's Capital City and the savages are the corporate executives.

BYRON C. LAMBERT

WHEN GEESE FLY SOUTH! is a magnificent story of indomitable determination against almost insurmountable odds. This book reads easily. The author writes with a literary flair and a responsible use of the Bible.

RICHARD PHILLIPS

Mesmerizing! Could not lay it down until I finished it. Many *holes* in my understanding were filled in and now make better sense.

RONNIE SAMS

This book gives great credit to God, prayer, and the *human spirit* as people seek to hold firm to their moral values and convictions.

RON SHEPHERD

The author is to be commended for hanging on during a bad situation.

GERALD STUCKEY

If the author had been covered with boils, he would rank with Job.

DAVID C. TINGLER

It arrested and held my attention from page one to the finish. What a strong message this book communicates on FIGHTING THE GOOD FIGHT OF FAITH!

CECIL TODD

A moving account of sacrifice and commitment to a mission and a message. . . . I had no idea about the anti-Christian bias in the Washington area. I pray that personal determination will be rewarded with continuing Mission support.

RICHARD WAMSLEY

It is an honest and unvarnished account of personal struggle. Read this book and weep. You keep reading, expecting to find a silver lining on the next page. What you find instead are more storm clouds.

LEONARD G. WYMORE

This book is a *must read* for those who have been lulled into thinking that all the real mission battles are overseas and not in our own country.

BOB STACY

It is a graphic example of what can happen to Christians when the Government or one of its agencies operates without restraint. To paraphrase a well-known Scripture, "Who knows but what this book has come to the Kingdom for such a time as this?"

RICHARD THROCKMORTON

Paul Benjamin

When Geese Fly South!

A Portrait of One Minister's Painful
Struggle With Banks & Bureaucracies

In Honor

of

Virginia Carol Vogel

by

Benjamin E. Vogel

"For God so loved the world that he gave his one and only Son, that whoso-ever believes in him shall not perish but have eternal life" (John 3:16 NIV).

Wild Geese

I hold to my heart when the geese are flying—
A wavering wedge on the high, bright blue—
I tighten my lips to keep from crying:
"Beautiful birds, let me go with you."

GRACE NOLL

PREFACE

WHEN GEESE FLY SOUTH! is written primarily as a tribute to the wonderful people called Partners who continued their friendship and encouragement during the darkest days of the National Church Growth Research Center. Their prayers and generosity turned defeat into victory.

I also wanted to give a first-hand account of the way that bureaucracy and corporate greed are choking the life out of our nation. While financial executives scramble each day to devise new and better ways of squeezing the public, the iron grip of the regulators grows tighter by the hour.

Lastly, I fervently wish to help some struggling preacher or other Christian leader to have the courage to persevere. Over the centuries, the laurels have gone to those who were willing to hang on a little longer.

Today, our basic freedoms as Americans are being tested in ways that have never occurred before in our national history. Someone has pointed out that we went to war with the British for far fewer regulations than we have now allowed to be imposed upon ourselves.

John Philpot Curran wrote, "The condition upon which God hath given liberty to man is eternal vigilance." Unless we become more acutely aware of what is happening in almost every community, we can lose every advantage for which the early patriots fought and died.

What lies ahead for Americans are generations of serfdom unless something can be done to roll back the tide of feudal aristocracy.

As citizens of the Kingdom of God, and Americans, it is time to look around. With prayerful hearts, we need to learn how to stand up for ourselves.

Paul Benjamin
Washington, D.C.
www.ncgrc.org

CONTENTS

I. EARLY STRUGGLES

II. THE CRUCIBLE

III. THE RESCUERS

IV. IN RETROSPECT

V. EPILOGUE

I.

Early Struggles

The love of liberty is the love of others;
the love of power is the love of ourselves.

Hazlitt

The effect of power and publicity in all men
is the aggravation of self, a sort of tumor
that ends up killing the victim's sympathies.

H. Adams

I. EARLY STRUGGLES

1. Briars and Brambles

When Andrew, our son, decided to find a nest of his own, he heard that Herndon, Virginia, was the place to look. We were living in Vienna, Virginia, at the time. Housing costs were less in Herndon, largely because it is ten miles farther out from the District of Columbia.

He toured several condominiums and decided that those concrete pillboxes were not for him. Then he discovered two acres of land just off Coral Road, one of the shortest streets in Herndon. This property was vacant with the exception of a two-storied white frame house that had been empty for five years.

The house was a disaster. Windows were shattered; plaster lay in piles on the floor, the living room was painted an ugly green, and the kitchen a garish pink. It was a long way from being anyone's "dream home" —more like a nightmare, actually.

Because trees, bushes, and tall grass surrounded the house, it was virtually invisible, both from Coral Road and Van Buren Street (the main artery of traffic). Some of the trees were magnificent. Five massive white oaks dominated the front yard. Even on the hottest days, you could sit on the front porch with comfort because of the cooling power of these behemoths.

Because of its seclusion, the old house made an ideal place for young people to meet and party. We picked up hundreds of beer cans. We also cleaned up syringes and hypodermic needles. The Herndon police were well aware of the address since they had made numerous drug raids there.

The owner was a salesperson at the local Oldsmobile dealership. He had bought the property with the idea of developing it; but now, double-digit interest rates were eating him up. He was willing to sell it on reasonable terms.

Although the house itself was in general disrepair, the frame was solid. It had been built in 1904 the old fashioned way. The studs and floor joists were oak. They were real "two-by-fours" and "two-by-tens" of a bygone building era, not the truncated versions found at the lumberyard today.

The oak frame had seasoned over the decades and had become like stone. You could not penetrate the studs with a common nail unless you drilled a hole first. Even then, the drill bit had to be sharp. Otherwise, you were forced to use a concrete nail. The house had another plus. The original metal roof was intact and did not leak.

It seemed to us that the land and the house had dramatic possibilities, even though the entire place had been badly neglected for many years. At the time, the National Church Growth Research Center was leasing office space on the tenth floor of the Honeywell Building in Tysons Corner, Virginia. This prestigious office area, located adjacent to the I-495 Beltway, has more rental space than downtown Miami. But it also has problems. It is heavily congested and rent was skyrocketing.

Because Andrew wanted a home and the Center needed additional space, working together in a partnership seemed the right course of action. Because of his skills in the building trades, he could restore the old house as a place to live. Since the front acre of the property was undeveloped, it offered an ideal building site for new offices. We would have the advantage of the appreciating value of our own property. In addition, our staff could avoid the traffic tie-ups at Tysons Corner.

We continued to pray about the matter and talk to our financial advisors. Because of the dip in the economy in 1981, the price seemed right. If we moved ahead with the purchase, we also had a hedge on the future. Our five-year lease was running out on the Honeywell Building. We would be in trouble if the landlord refused to let us stay. If we came up with the down payment on Coral Road, the owner was willing to provide the financing.

We put the settlement date the first week in June. Meanwhile, we were anxious to get started with the cleanup. We secured permission from the owner to start work on Memorial Day, several days before we concluded the transaction.

Memorial Day, 1981, was bright and beautiful. The temperature was in the low seventies. A gentle breeze was blowing, as it usually did in the summer from the west. We donned our oldest work clothes. Lois had prepared a delicious lunch.

We worked all day, hauling out fallen plaster and broken glass in five-gallon buckets. Blackberry bushes, taller than a grown person, completely dominated the back yard close to the house. They did not want to be disturbed. They took their revenge with lacerations all over your body. You paid for their removal with your own blood.

In spite of the hard work, the crew that was helping seemed to be having a great time. We were laughing and joking with each other all day.

We enjoyed getting away from the office for a little while into "God's great outdoors." In spite of our labors, we barely made a dent in the cleanup. But at least, now we could walk across the living room floor with far less risk of being cut by glass or impaled by a drug needle. The future looked as rosy as the dawn.

Driving back to Vienna that night, we were sunburned and exhausted. No one seemed to care. We had experienced a really "fun" day. But looking back now, if we could have gazed into a crystal ball and viewed the calamity that was coming, our laughter would have turned to tears.

2. A House of Prayer

One of our goals in moving to Washington was to help plant new churches. The second Sunday we were in town, Lois and I transferred our membership to a new congregation that was meeting in a high school in Alexandria. Because they did not have a full-time minister, I was asked to help out with the preaching.

Over the next year and a half, I preached for this new church on an average of every other Sunday. The remaining time, we were traveling, usually involved in Faith-Promise Rallies, Church Growth Seminars, and other similar meetings. Finally, the church called its own minister.

Because we wanted to let our Partners know what their mission dollars were doing, we mentioned on several occasions that we were involved in "helping" to plant a new church in the Washington Metro area. Later on, we were shocked and surprised when some of the new leaders told us that we were to refrain from mentioning our part in their church since we had hardly been there. The letter stated that we were guilty of misinformation.

Lois went back to our records and sent a documented list of all the Sundays I had preached, along with some of our calling nights. She did not mention the hours I had spent in counseling. Why did the leadership that emerged want to deny any involvement of the National Church Growth Research Center? What did they have to gain by denying the truth of what happened? We were incredulous!

Meanwhile, Andrew had started a Bible Study in Vienna with a number of unchurched young people. For the most part, they had dropped through the cracks of religious institutions. They were suspicious of churches, but at the same time, they were not sure that Christianity did not have something to offer.

During this same period of time, we were able to baptize our next-door neighbor. Sue was an earnest seeker. Once she gave her heart to the Lord, she wanted to learn everything she could about the Christian life. I directed her to the *Oxford Annotated Bible* as a study tool and she spent hours with it every day. We also met weekly in a one-to-one study hour to discuss my book *Christian Growth*. She was a delightful disciple. On Sunday afternoons, we met in her home along with her friends and relatives for a Bible Study.

We decided to merge our two Bible Study groups and find a place to meet. Herndon seemed like the logical place. We investigated a funeral home and the upstairs room of the Herndon Volunteer Fire

Department. They did not want us. We could not afford to rent office space. The only place left was the old house on our newly acquired Coral Road property.

With the paint peeling off outside and the plaster falling inside, the Old House was not exactly a textbook place to launch a new Bible Study. But since we were unable to find any other location that suited our budget, it seemed to be our only choice.

Our only choice turned out to be the right choice. Sue and her family began meeting with us on Sunday morning along with the young people from Andrew's youth group. Everyone loved the secluded atmosphere. We devoted Sunday mornings to worship and Sunday afternoons to clean up. After a communal lunch (people born and raised in this area had never heard the term "potluck"), we sallied forth with mowers and sickles to conquer the underbrush and grass that was up to our shoulders.

We turned the land into a green oasis in the middle of a desert of concrete and asphalt. We had a veritable animal farm. Deer, woodchucks, foxes, feral cats, moles, opossums, raccoons—they all found refuge on our property. As the blacktop spread and commercial buildings multiplied, so did our menagerie.

Now instead of briars, thorn trees, and crabgrass, a lush green lawn emerged. Wild daisies, violets, and Virginia bluebonnets began to appear. An ugly duckling became a swan. The "Front Acre" became our athletic field. We enjoyed softball, badminton, croquet, and our favorite—volleyball.

The thicket outside could be remedied, but the Old House was a basket case. It needed more than a facelift; it needed major surgery. The job of remodeling was by no means insurmountable, but it was costly and required more money than we could afford. Consequently, we had to get along the best way we could.

Our attendance for Bible Study began to grow. Those who joined us were enthusiastically telling others about a "unique church" in Herndon. They came on Sunday morning bringing their friends. We were soon running out of space. We spent our first Thanksgiving knocking out the non-bearing wall between the living room and the dining room.

Lois was in charge of the music and Andrew and I divided the preaching between us. The worship atmosphere was spontaneous and relaxed. Because the acoustics were so good, our singing sounded like a congregation of two hundred or more. I felt free and uninhibited during my preaching. Our informal setting helped to take away the "on-the-spot feeling" that usually accompanies preaching in a formal church service or bringing an address at a major convention.

Someone has pointed out that many people experience pleasure in this life, but that few people find real joy. Those of us who were meeting at Coral Road were having a ball. We could hardly wait until Sunday rolled around. I was reminded of Luke's testimony about the new Christians meeting in Jerusalem, who "partook of food with glad and generous hearts, praising God and having favor with all the people. And the Lord added to their number day by day those who were being saved" (Acts 2:46-47).

Coral Road had its moments of good-natured humor. A persistent swarm of bees had constructed a hive just inside the front door. We tried insecticides and brooms but we only succeeded in getting stung for our efforts. For a while, we told everyone coming on Sunday morning to enter by the back door. Otherwise, we could not insure their safety. Those who did leave by the front door were like the folks in most churches today—they did not linger long.

We also had tragedy. I met Bill B. at the health club in Tysons Corner. He was a physical therapist. While he worked on my back (an old injury from a college student-faculty softball game), I worked on his soul. I told him about our group meeting at Coral Road. Bill was skeptical. He did not want to become involved with some cult.

Bill had grown up in Maryland in an upper-class home. His mother had taken him at a tender age to Sunday School at the nearby Episcopal church. But like so many young people in the sixties, Bill was caught up in the hippie movement. A heart-wrenching divorce made him think about the kind of life he wanted now. Also, he had the custody of his beautiful daughter, Antara. Bill keenly felt his responsibility as a parent. He wanted her to have a better life.

One Sunday morning, Bill drove up our long lane at Coral Road in his pickup. He brought Antara and his huge red retriever named **19**

Loose with him. Bill was handsome and charming. Our folks loved him from the start. He had a magnificent bass voice. Lois urged him to sing a solo. He was reluctant at first, but finally, he agreed to sing "Holy, Holy, Holy"—his favorite hymn.

Bill never sang for us. The following week, he and Antara both burned to death in a mysterious fire. Some speculated that the fire had been deliberately set and was drug-related, perhaps going back to Bill's earlier life. Nothing was ever proven. Whatever the circumstances, our loss was searing.

Ironically, Bill was a distant relative of a tugboat captain who now was worth millions because of wise investments. The captain had no close heirs, and Bill was in line to receive a vast inheritance.

After we became friends, he told me one day about his good fortune. He said that once the money was his, the National Church Growth Research Center would never be in financial need. One of his first projects, he said, would be to help us put a new office building on our Coral Road property. We often thought of the "might-have-beens" when in later years we were going through such a desperate financial struggle because of the Banks and the County.

3. Wooden Men with Iron Sticks

Our Bible Study group at Coral Road had been operating for several months in a carefree atmosphere. We were glad to be living in the United States of America where the First Amendment guaranteed our religious freedom. We did not realize what a rocky road lay ahead for us.

One of our first concerns at Coral Road was to replace the broken panes. Since many of the frames were falling apart, we decided to set in new windows. I had met a lumberman through the American Festival of Evangelism. He was willing to ship us new Anderson windows at cost. Andrew began tearing out the old frames and installing new ones.

When he was out for lunch one day, Mr. P., the Herndon Building Inspector, came up our lane in his town pickup and began snooping.

When Andrew returned, Mr. P. had posted bright red "STOP WORK" signs everywhere! When Andrew walked into our house, Mr. P. assailed him. He asked angrily, "What right do you have to replace these windows without a Construction Permit?" Andrew replied defensively that he did not know he needed one. Mr. P. assured him that he did.

Andrew decided to cooperate and drove over to the town headquarters. He stood in a long line for an hour or more before he could get to the clerk. The lady in charge checked over his application forms and gave him the permit. He was amazed at how much it cost just to get permission to replace a few windows.

Andrew put in the new frames, but the end was not yet. The Old House had a brick chimney. Because the original mortar was deteriorating, bricks were sliding down the metal roof and hitting the ground. We were afraid that someone would get conked on the head. Every Sunday after worship, we stacked the bricks that had fallen during the week.

Turning his attention now to the chimney, Andrew began systematically lifting out the old bricks. He left to grab a bite to eat, and once again when he returned, Mr. P.'s official truck was in the driveway. As before, the bright red "STOP WORK" orders were everywhere. This time, Mr. P. was even more incensed. What did Andrew think he was doing, taking out loose bricks without a Demolition Permit? Since it was, after all, "our property," Andrew was flabbergasted to think that he needed a permit to do what common sense directed. But as someone has pointed out, "The problem with common sense is that it is not too common."

Again, Andrew went over to the Town Offices to stand in line with dozens of other permit seekers. He made an application for a Demolition Permit in triplicate. Finally, the lady at the window responded to his needs. She charged him another fee that seemed exorbitant for the small job he had to do. But now he could go back to removing the bricks, "legally."

While he was talking to the clerk, Andrew inquired about buying the Building Code Book for the County known as BOCA. "After all," he said, "I want to keep up with the regulations." The woman was hesitant. She told Andrew that the book was several inches thick and cost a great deal of money. Andrew persisted. He said he did not want to keep coming back because of some obscure rule he did not know about. Finally, she said with some exasperation, "We don't have any Code Books here, and besides, if we did, it won't do you any good to own one. The Code Book only means what the Building Inspector says it means." Mr. P., it seems, was "entrenched in his own infallibility."

It was obvious from the outset that Mr. P.'s heart was not filled with daisies and buttercups. Later on, we learned more about his zeal as a Town Official. A friend of ours who worked in real estate told us that if Mr. P. suspected that you were remodeling your basement without the proper permits, he had been known to come around to the back of your home and peer into the basement through the window wells. If he saw signs of improvements, he issued a citation from the Town and threatened you with legal action.

Mr. P. was only the tip of the iceberg as far as regulators were concerned. You would have thought we were constructing a fourteen-story office building in Tysons Corner. Bureaucratic officials from a dozen different agencies kept coming on our property. The problem with our times, as someone has pointed out, is that "Iron men with wooden sticks have been replaced by wooden men with iron sticks."

4. Yearning to Breathe Free

For a long time, we could not believe what our eyes and ears were telling us. Were we living in the America that Emma Lazarus sang about when she penned:

> Give me your tired, your poor,
> Your huddled masses yearning to breathe free?

It seemed that we had been transported to some foreign country, governed by a dictator who was in charge of every aspect of our life.

We learned that the Town of Herndon was actually lax in enforc-

ing its regulations when compared with Reston, our next-door neighbor. Reston was a planned community from the beginning. Not only do you have the Town Rules, you also have a strict Home-owner's Association. Houses all over the city are color-coded. You cannot even change the shade of paint on your front door without permission from the powers that be.

One evening Lois and I were enjoying a TV documentary on Alaska. The couple being interviewed were building their own home on a small farm they had purchased. When the media spokesperson asked them how they liked living there, they said it was wonderful. The couple pointed to their home under construction and said how happy they were not to be hounded by government officials breath-ing down their necks. "Where did you live before?" the interviewer asked. The husband looked off in the distance for a moment and then sighed, "Reston, Virginia."

Meanwhile, at our offices in the high-rise Honeywell Building in Tysons Corner, we were rapidly running out of space. One of our Special Projects was the American Festival of Evangelism. Because of the encouragement of Donald McGavran and other worthies in the Church Growth realm, we decided to preserve the materials that had emerged from that historic event.

We began working on four Festival Notebooks that carried the manuscripts of all the major speeches as well as the two hundred Workshops. To our knowledge, nothing like this effort had ever been attempted before. We planned to make all manuscripts reproducible so that teachers in Sunday Schools or professors in Colleges could duplicate what they needed without copyright infringement. We printed a million manuscripts and if conservatively speaking, each manuscript was copied only one hundred times, then there would be one hundred million manuscripts on every phase of evangelism cir-culating around the globe.

These manuscripts required a much larger storage facility than we had available in Tysons Corner. Since we had room for expansion at Coral Road, it made sense to us to put up some kind of modest building rather than lease more space at exorbitant prices. We called our building the "Mail Room," since we planned to use it for our nationwide mailings.

A couple in our church who had come out of the hippie culture designed the Mail Room. When it came to woodworking, Dan and Linda could make anything. As an expression of their gratitude for the warmth and love they found in our Bible Study Group, they wanted to build something unique.

Dan and Linda liked plenty of light. They surrounded the building with large windows and put specially designed half-round windows as the crown of each frame. The round windows were custom made in their own shop. In a two-story building where the footprint was just twelve hundred square feet, we had sixteen large windows and four smaller ones. No problem with light for us.

Since we had run into trouble with the Town of Herndon on the Old House, we decided to do everything "according to Hoyle" on the Mail Room. As the building was going up, we had to have a town inspection on each phase before we could move to the next. Each time an inspector came by, he left behind a trail of new stickers with an illegible set of initials on the bottom line. In the end, we had nine inspections for a building that the Town was labeling a "garage."

One of the area builders who had been around the block a few times counseled us, "If you want to pass inspections," he said, "put out a case of Budweiser and leave. When you return, the Budweiser will be gone, but you will be approved." We did not follow through on his idea.

With so much red tape wrapped around us everywhere we turned, we had a difficult time "breathing free" in our American homeland. In fact, we were suffocating from bureaucratic smog.

5. Getting the Boot

After our first go-around with the Town, we decided to keep our profile as low as possible. We did not take out ads in the paper or buy radio spots. All information about our Bible Study Group was by word of mouth.

We continued to take precautions. After our meetings on Sunday morning, we stacked all the chairs and put them in a side room without low windows. The Center inherited a number of cloth pennants from the American Festival of Evangelism. These banners had been hung around the auditorium in Kansas City to make the occasion more festive. Now we used them to stop prying eyes from peering through the windows. We also installed deadbolts and window locks. If any more snooping was going on, we did not want to give the intruders easy access.

One of our members had a connection for seafood at the Maine Avenue Wharf in the District of Columbia. He would get up early on some Sundays and bring back several bushels of blue crabs. While we were singing, the crabs were simmering in a huge iron kettle in the front yard under the oak trees. After services, we went outside to enjoy a crab feast and, later on, some great volleyball.

As the Mail Room began to take shape, we were glad to have the prospects of more space. By now, our Bible Study Group was over-flowing the Old House. Not only were we filling up the living and dining room, we were also crowding into the kitchen and pantry. On many Sundays, we had people sitting on the steps leading upstairs.

Another reason why we were glad to have the prospects of the Mail Room was because Mr. P. said the house was unsafe. Because it was so old, he said, it could tumble down at any time. Later on, several structural engineers told us that because of our seasoned oak frame, we had one of the safest buildings in town. One architect said that if a hurricane came through, we would have one of the few buildings left standing.

Mr. P. also said we had termites. We called a licensed extermi-nator who gave us a clean bill of health. When we conveyed this information to Mr. P., he was still adamant—his report said we had termites, so we had termites! Alas, Caesar had spoken.

When the Mail Room was finally finished, we all rejoiced. Now we could all be together on one floor and not scattered all over the Old House. We spent the next week cleaning up the dust and debris and mopping the concrete floor in the new building. Then we brought over the chairs and piano from the Old House. Our lectern was a large music stand. At last, we had a structure that had been fully approved by the Town and the County. We thought about turning the piano to the wall and hiding the chairs. With our recently approved facilities, such a procedure did not seem necessary. We were dead wrong.

When Andrew came out to Coral Road that week to mow, he saw Mr. P.'s dreaded pickup in the driveway along with another official looking car. This time Mr. P. had brought reinforcements—one of the top Zoning Officials from F-County. They had been peeping through the windows of the Mail Room. They were angry and rude, "cold in authority, haughty in self-assurance."

They accused us of erecting a church instead of a garage. When Andrew insisted that it was a garage, the zoning official retorted, "Well, it looks like a church to me." Then he went on, "I've never seen a garage with round windows." "Yes," Andrew responded, "but did you ever see a church with sixteen foot doors?" Then, he laughed. The visitors were not amused.

"It is illegal for you to have a church here because of parking issues," said one authority. Andrew answered by saying that we were not having a church but a Bible Study. "Furthermore," he said, "we have plenty of off-street parking, and therefore, we are not causing any traffic problems for our neighbors."

Andrew mentioned the millions of dollars that F-County was pouring into drug rehabilitation. He told them that some of the same young people who had used Coral Road as a drug haven were now substance free. They had been baptized and were attending our Bible Study.

Later, my son reported that he felt as though he was talking to a brick wall. The officials turned a deaf ear to anything he was saying. But the end was not yet. We were getting the boot. The Herndon police had already been notified. If they saw our cars again on Sunday, they had orders to take us off our property with force.

We called an emergency meeting of our Bible Study Group and prayed fervently about our next move. Some were crying; others were angry. We did not believe what was happening. We were not hurting anyone; we were not bothering anyone: it all seemed so unfair. Someone asked if we were living in Washington or Moscow. Another individual suggested that USA should be changed to USSA—

the United Socialist States of America. The People's Republic of Herndon was mentioned several times.

Ironically, just around the corner from us on Eldon Street was a hard-rock music store that operated out of a house. Many of our young people knew that this place, called the Peacock Feather, was also a drug hangout. If you had the name of the right person, you could buy all kinds of drugs and the paraphernalia to go along with them. The County had made a colossal error: they had shut down the wrong place! It was Jonathan Swift, the Irish writer and church-man, who wrote:

> Laws are like cobwebs, which may catch small flies,
> but let wasps and hornets break through.

We agonized about what to do next. We remembered the pic-tures of students standing in front of tanks in Hungary. We thought about meeting on Sunday morning as usual, *but this time,* tipping off the media. Then, some of our Bible Study members would lie down on the driveway in front of the police cars while reporters had their cameras running.

The more we appraised our situation, the less sanguine we felt about getting a fair shake from a "liberal media." In all probability, the media would come down on the side of the County. Then the tut-tutting would begin. What can you expect from a society when even churches think that they can break the law and get away with it!

Actually, we were not violating any rules since F-County allows a Bible Study Group to meet at a residential site. But we reasoned that by the time the reporters did their spin, the general public would not know truth from fiction. We decided against turning our situa-tion over to their "inventive genius." Abraham Lincoln said that he never read the newspapers because, "First they lied, and then they re-lied."

We decided that even going to court did not hold much promise of reprieve. Courts mean lawyers and lawyers cost money. F-County keeps a battery of high-priced lawyers at their disposal. The County could afford to keep the battle running until Armageddon. We would be lucky to afford one day.

Among our Founding Fathers, no one was more fearful that the New Republic would turn despotic than Thomas Jefferson. During his travels in Europe, he witnessed the plight of ordinary citizens being ground into the dirt by an autocratic state. Jefferson felt that "Men are more important than constitutions, and the public well-being is more sacred than statutes."

The statesman from Monticello was afraid that "gradualism" would erode the liberties won from the British at the cost of blood. According to Vernon Louis Parrington, Jefferson saw clearly that the greater the power of government, the ampler its revenues, the more energetic its administration, *the more dangerous it may become to the rights of men.* We felt that we were enduring in microcosm what Jefferson feared most.

In a moment of cold realism, we knew that our "mad marvelous independence was gone" and probably would never return. Big Brother was watching!

6. On The Road Again

Our Bible Study had begun as a migratory group. Now we were on the road again without a home of our own. F-County and the Town had taken away our nesting site. We loved our meeting place at Coral Road, but we could not stay there without going to war with one of the richest and most powerful counties in the United States.

Because we were about ten minutes from Dulles International Airport, our entire area is saturated with hotels and motels. Surely, we thought, we can find a place to meet in one of them. We could, but the arrangement also had a hitch.

Motel managers were willing to rent us meeting space on a Sunday-by-Sunday basis—no long-term contracts. The reason was simple. They often had unreserved meeting rooms on Sunday morning. On the other hand, the managers never knew when they would be booking a group that needed every available room. Under those circumstances, we would have been a nuisance.

In the summer of 83, we began bouncing back and forth from

one motel to another. On one Sunday, we met at the Reston Sheraton; the next Sunday, you could find us at the Holiday Inn or the Dulles Airport Marriott. These surroundings were decidedly upscale from the Old House at Coral Road.

We never had been a "dress up" group. I always wore a suit and tie as a carryover from my mother's influence. Schooled in Bethany College under W. R. Walker and S. S. Lappin, she felt that the dignity of the pulpit demanded that a minister should look his best.

Our young people did not have the same sort of compulsion. They came in faded shirts and holey blue jeans. We did not make dress an issue. We believed that the presence of the young people and their willingness to listen to the Word of God superseded everything else.

The Dulles Marriott was generous to us. They granted us the use of a plush meeting room that often was used by high-powered Washington executives and, sometimes, world leaders. A lush red carpet was accented by elegant drapes. Overhead, a huge chandelier, brilliantly lighted, dominated the ceiling. A silver coffee and tea service graced a corner of our room.

For a place that was usually thronged by expensive blue suits, our group looked as though they came from another planet. We wondered if the spiffy attendants were saying to themselves, "Who are these people and whence have they come?" The truth is, many of our young people came from some of the most affluent homes in the area. They were independent about their dress just as they were independent about everything else in their lives.

We did not mind the upscale treatment we were receiving from the hotels and motels. Our problem was logistics and communication. Sometimes a manager could not tell us until the middle of the week whether or not he would have space available for the following Sunday. Glitches in communication were bound to occur. On several Sundays, we would be meeting at one motel while other members of our group would be waiting somewhere else. Since these sessions predated today's ubiquitous cell phone, we had no way of touching base.

Someone told us that our old nemesis, F-County, allowed outside groups to meet in public schools, so long as the price was right. We wanted to stay as far away from the County as possible, but we concluded that because of the unsatisfactory motel situation, we really did not have another option.

Andrew and another appointee from our fellowship decided to visit an administrator with the County. He was the one responsible for leasing space to outside groups. When Andrew and his friend were finally ushered into his office, the school representative was "proud as Lucifer and as cold as a lizard."

The official wanted to know who we were. Andrew told him that we were a part of the Christian Church. The man said he had never heard of the "Christian Church." He wondered if we were a cult. Andrew replied that on the contrary, our religious roots went all the way back to the New Testament. He tried to give him a brief synopsis of the Restoration Movement. Far from being a cult, he said, we are a group that is trying to preach and practice the simple religion of the early church.

The matter of church finances came up. The school representative strongly suspected that Andrew and I were a couple of hirelings who were out to fleece the flock. Andrew replied that we were not even being paid a salary for our services. Still the "cult idea" lingered. Somehow, the man could not get the idea out of his brain.

What happened next belongs to the theater of the absurd! The school representative then asked if we held revival meetings and called in outside evangelists. Andrew replied that up to now, we had not scheduled any evangelistic meetings. Then the school official said, "When you do get an outside speaker, we want him to be from F-County so the money will be spent here." Andrew and our other appointee were speechless!

Finally, after a prolonged thrust-and-parry session, the official said that he would make the Herndon Elementary School available. Our lease was for only two hours on Sunday morning and if we ran over, even a few minutes beyond the allotted time, we would be charged for another full hour. In addition, the custodian received (as I recall) forty-five dollars hourly. His fees would also increase if we exceeded our two-hour limit.

When Andrew and our representative stood to leave, the County official said menacingly, "Just remember, I'll be watching you." Andrew said later that he felt as though he was the head of some terrorist organization that was about to poison the city water supply.

With our new lease with the Public Schools, we were now paying more in rent than the cost of the mortgage at Coral Road. We already had a place to meet that did not cost us any additional monies. But the Regulators did not seem the least bit bothered about our financial struggles. As far as they were concerned, we could pay the freight or go out of business. It made no difference to them.

At least, for the time being our distress about space was over. We met in the school cafeteria that seats over eight hundred students. You could only reach the cafeteria after walking down a long and cheerless corridor. Once you arrived, the room swallowed you up. Our group of forty or fifty souls met down front in one corner. But the whole place did not seem right. We were the unwelcome guests in the house of a stranger.

Some of our newer young people began to slip away. They loved the novelty and closeness of our meeting place at Coral Road. They could not feel at home in a place that could double as a roller skating rink.

For those of us who had grown up in the faith, we resented our circumstances, but we knew that the building is not the church. But as someone has pointed out, "First we shape our architecture and then our architecture shapes us." Coral Road had provided a warm and close atmosphere for our fellowship. Now that setting had been forcibly removed. Fledglings in the faith were fleeing.

7. A Tall Refuge

The tallest structure in the historic district of downtown Herndon was dedicated by the Methodists in 1915. Covered with blond bricks and crowned by a graceful spire, many people see this edifice as a striking piece of turn-of-the-century architecture. The Methodists put on an addition in 1940, and then in 1955, they built a three-story educational wing. The building is located on two acres of prime real estate.

To Lois and me, the building was reminiscent of the town and country church buildings of our youth. Our preacher fathers had served congregations whose meeting places were almost identical. We had a twinge of nostalgia every time we drove by the Methodist structure.

When we learned that the Methodists were moving to the edge of the town and selling their building, the situation seemed opportune, both for the Center and the Church. Now that we were meeting in a public facility, our Bible Study Group had become Community Christian Church.

Our thoughts about building a new facility on the front acre at Coral Road had dimmed in view of our negative experiences in constructing a Mail Room. If that simple structure required nine inspections, who knows how many hoops we would need to jump through in order to put up a major building.

We already had some idea of the red tape involved from the experiences of other churches. We knew that in F-County, from the time a congregation first begins to meet until they get into their own building, the waiting period averages fourteen years—one of the longest time-spans in the nation.

Other Christian Churches in the area had already been through building nightmares. One congregation had to submit their blueprints to the County seven times because their plans kept disappearing. They strongly suspected that some of the county planners who hated churches were deliberately foiling their efforts. Another congregation had a building lot in the shape of a pentagon. The owners on four sides gladly gave their permission to build. On the fifth side, a lady whose land abutted the church boundary line just a short distance vetoed the idea.

We were always contending with a hostile attitude, usually unspoken, which downgraded churches and their usefulness in a materialistic world. Much of the problem related to money. The county bureaucracy, always greedy for more tax dollars, casts a baleful eye upon real estate that is tax-exempt. In a small town where an acre brings five to ten thousand dollars, the tax consequences are small. But in an area where one acre sells for a million dollars or more, the County sees good tax revenue going up in smoke.

We sensed that churches are on the bottom of the institutional totem pole. Public schools are fine; hospitals are fine; community centers are fine; parks are fine. After all, they make a contribution to the betterment of society. But churches are a different breed. Their talk of "pie in the sky by and by" serves no earthly good. In a county bureaucracy where thousands of employees hold degrees from "liberal universities," churches and other religious organizations tend to be downgraded as relics of past superstitions.

As a case in point, a beautiful red brick church building was located on three acres of land in the heart of Tysons Corner. Situated in the midst of commercial buildings and one of the largest shopping malls in America, many of us saw this church as a symbol of our nation's real hope. At Christmas when the whole area became an engine for the god of commercialism, it was comforting to hear the church carillon sounding out familiar hymns and Christmas carols.

Meanwhile, developers who coveted the land for their own purposes were bombarding the leaders of the congregation. The newspapers picked up the story. They gave it front-page treatment. The editors concluded that this church was occupying valuable real estate that should be put to better use—i.e., more shops and office buildings.

For a long time, a few stout-hearted souls in the congregation held out for the idea of a Christian witness in an area of high visibility. In the long run, the commercial interests won. The congregation relocated to the suburbs where as one writer put it, "churches belong." Someone has pointed out that in Europe, the cathedral stands at the heart of the city, whereas in America, the sports stadium and shopping mall now occupy that coveted position.

Reading between the lines on this front-page story, as well as drawing on my own experience, I concluded that non-Christian people do not want to feel uncomfortable in the presence of church spires and Christian crosses. So therefore, construct your churches away from the mainstream—build them on back roads and cul-de-sacs. We better not make anyone feel uneasy by putting religious symbols in the marketplace!

As time went on, the Methodist church became more and more attractive to us. Because of strict building codes along with innumerable zoning restrictions, over two hundred congregations in F-County do not have a home of their own. Vacant church buildings are "scarcer than hen's teeth." We knew that the Methodist building would not be on the market for long. Since it was already "there," our financial advisors felt it would be prudent to make a bid.

We were bolstered in our thinking by a booming economy. The "trickle down" monetary theory, derided by so many Ivy League economists in the eighties, was beginning to take hold. With fewer taxes to pay, businesses had more money for research and development. Real estate prices in Washington were soaring, especially around Dulles International Airport. The price of land was going up monthly.

Our Coral Road property was surrounded by thirty-five acres of prime commercial land. Because we jutted into the heart of the entire parcel (called a "spike" in real estate jargon), we had a commanding presence. The cost of building around us or ignoring our acreage would be enormous. A few commercial developers, thinking that a church group would have no real estate savvy, tried to snatch up our land for peanuts. When they realized that we were not the dumbest kid on the block, they began to take us more seriously.

Some of the verbal offers on Coral Road began to approach a million dollars. Meanwhile, we learned that our old nemesis, F-County, was our chief contender in buying the Methodist Church. County officials had plans to turn the building into a government childcare center. They also wanted to erect low-rent housing units on the land surrounding the building.

As the meringue on the pie, the County would be operating on property that was already tax-exempt. If they built elsewhere, they would be removing highly assessed property from their tax rolls.

After praying diligently about the matter and consulting with our financial advisors, we decided to offer a bid for the Methodist Church. Although Coral Road had not sold at this point, we knew that if we waited any longer, the Methodist building would be gone. With the offers that we were now getting on Coral Road, we could pay off the Methodist building in cash and still put away several hundred thousand dollars in a Trust Fund for emergencies.

The County upped the bid we made for the Methodist building.

An unscrupulous real estate agent, sensing he would get a larger commission if he steered the building to the County, was secretly working against us. Upon the advice of our financial counselors, we decided to raise our offer. We knew that we would not last long in a bidding war with F-County.

We had a strong ally in Dr. Purnell Bailey, a retired Methodist District Superintendent. Dr. Bailey and I became good friends during the national Key 73 evangelistic campaign. Our cause was helped also by a Methodist widow who had been present for the corner-stone laying of the original building. She did not want the church to go to the County. She wanted to see it continue as a house of prayer. She buttonholed every one of the Methodist leaders and said, "If you vote to sell our building to the County, you are not my friend."

In the end, the building was ours. We could not believe it! Every other encounter with the County had ended in our bloody withdrawal. We were amused at the local papers that took up a familiar theme—what a shame that this valuable downtown piece of real estate could not have been put to better use. But by now, we had been around the mulberry bush so many times in a secular society, we knew better than to expect a fair shake from the media.

We now owned two valuable properties in an area where real estate values were climbing every day. But we also had two mortgages. Our payment on Coral Road had sharply increased since we had to leverage that property in order to buy the Methodist building.

It seemed for a while that all our prayers were being answered. We were now buying property instead of leasing. The Methodist building had enough space to house the National Church Growth Research Center and Community Christian Church.

Unlike the elementary school where we had to carry all our church furniture in for Sunday services and then carry it all out again, we had a beautiful sanctuary for worship. We could lock the door and leave the pulpit and the pews behind. Furthermore, we did not have to pay overtime to a janitor. With Lois playing the piano, Doris at the organ, and Nelva singing solos, our music was heaven-sent. The acoustics were excellent. How wonderful it was to be worshipping God again under our own roof.

We were putting the Methodist building to good use. Our books and other evangelistic resources were circling the globe. We had our own first-class print shop. A sequel for the American Festival of Evangelism was being planned for Chicago. We were chosen to coordinate this major event. It was to be called Congress 88.

Without our newly acquired facilities, we did not have the space to lead a project of that magnitude. The decisions we had made seemed to be fully justified by the use we were getting out of our properties. We felt that the scope of our Christian witness had been greatly increased with a strong potential for even greater service in the Kingdom. We sang with Robert Browning:

> God's in his heaven—
> All's right with the world!

8. The Hammerstroke

From outward appearances, our financial situation in the fall of 88 was an enviable one. A beautiful structure was in our name in a County where available church buildings are a rarity. We also had two contracts on our Coral Road property. The first contract, eighty pages long, was with a national public storage company. The second backup contract was with a well-established lumberyard in Tysons Corner. They were interested in expanding their business in the high-growth area known as the Dulles Corridor, with Herndon as the center of their operations.

Although numerous potential buyers had expressed a verbal interest in the Coral Road property, no purchaser up to this point had offered us an actual contract. These agreements were the first that included earnest money and we signed both of them.

What happened over the next few months is still unbelievable to many people who live in other parts of the nation. The rumblings we were hearing about a downturn in the economy were nothing new. We had heard them before. Every business cycle has its bulls and bears. And, someone has added, its "pigs"!

The real estate market is close to the heart of the economy. Some fiscal scholars say, "real estate is the heart." Politicians and developers have courted each other for years. But even the talk about the market "going south" did not prepare the business community for what happened next. The economy not only went "south," it began a precipitous downward spiral. Many were calling it "the crash."

During the next year, the majority of builders in Washington went out of business. The developers working around our Coral Road property all declared bankruptcy. We were the only ones to survive. Many companies had executives on their staff with the coveted Master of Business Administration degree from Harvard University. These were the people who were supposed to have a real handle on what was going on in the economy. They went under, also. The bulls on Wall Street were turning into bears.

Now, instead of a real estate broker on your doorstep wanting to buy your property, they were closing up shop in droves. Buyers for commercial property were virtually nonexistent. The well heeled were waiting for liquidation opportunities. The whole area was overbuilt; it would take years to utilize all the available space.

Real estate developers use the expression, "see-through space." It is their shorthand for open areas in commercial buildings that are not leased. Lois and I took our late-night walks with Duchess, my German Shepherd and Pup-Pup, Lois's Pekinese, around the empty buildings near Coral Road that had more than a million square feet of vacant space.

Many people living in the Midwest could not comprehend the severity of the "crash" in eastern real estate. Although farmland in the central states eroded in price, it still held much of its earlier value. In our part of the country, buyers were wary of commercial land.

Real estate developers were scrambling to get out of signed contracts. The seller could file suit, but by the time your case came to court, the buyer had already declared bankruptcy. Meanwhile, you would be saddled with thousands of dollars in attorney fees.

With shots coming from all directions, we were now flying a tattered flag. Instead of the Center being out of debt, we owed more money than ever. Although we were barely able to eke out the mortgages on the church and Coral Road, we were comforted by the knowledge that we would someday be out of financial bondage. The sale of Coral Road was our key to financial freedom.

But now the key was stuck in a rusty lock. We had the melancholy prospects of paying double mortgages for a long time to come. Our financial advisors tried to cheer us. "Look," they said, "financial markets have always had their ups and downs. It is just a matter of time. Be patient and everything will work out all right."

With two huge mortgages staring us in the face every month, that information did not brighten our day. All we could think about was, "How are we going to make it?" Later on, when it turned out that we were the only people around Coral Road to survive bankruptcy, someone quipped, "They trusted in Harvard; you trusted in heaven"!

II.
The
Crucible

The power to tax is the power to destroy.

Marshall

That government is best which governs least.

Thoreau

II. THE CRUCIBLE

1. Adrift in the Wind

When Lois and I began talking seriously about moving to Washington, D.C., we looked for a location that was convenient to both National and Dulles airports. The maps indicated that Vienna, Virginia, was halfway between them.

I was traveling almost every week, not only for the Center, but also for the American Festival of Evangelism and later, Congress 88. Sometimes my schedule was so tight, I barely made it between airports. I often caught the "redeye" flight from Los Angeles to Dulles. Lois stayed up the rest of the night washing my clothes and repacking my suitcase while I caught a few extra winks. Then I would head out for National to get a "sunrise" flight.

The house we purchased in Vienna was a split-level with four bedrooms. We used the ground-floor family room as my study. We converted part of the second floor into a "mother-in-law apartment" so my mom could come and live with us.

The locale was conducive to study and writing. Behind our home, five terraces sloped down to a fence that bordered ninety-acre woods in the heart of Vienna. Our agent told us that the wooded area was a gift to the city from a wealthy benefactor. The will stipulated that it could never be developed.

Although we loved our Vienna home, our financial situation was growing more grim every day. To help ease the burden, we were able to secure some small loans from individuals. (Later on, a few of these notes turned into some of our worst torment.) We still needed more help. The relentless pressure of two large mortgages necessitated some drastic action.

After much prayer, Lois and I decided to sell our home and make those funds available to the Center. Although we looked upon the transaction as a loan, we did not know if we would ever see the money again. We realized that others who had a claim on the Center would have to be taken care of first.

We signed up with a real estate agent and put our house on the market. With its excellent location close to the Vienna Metro Station, it should have been gone in a few weeks. But with the real estate situation so flat, nearly a year would go by before we signed the settlement papers.

Under normal circumstances, buying a home in the Washington area is one of the best investments you can make. Houses appreciate at a rate that is better than the national average. It is not uncommon for a house to double its value every five years. The equity in our Vienna home was supposed to be our retirement monies. Not only were we giving up a place to live, we were also trading on our future.

The only place left for us was the Old House on Coral Road. When we bought that property, the house was appraised for one thousand dollars. All the value was in the land. We had already made some improvements to the house, but it still did not have heat and electricity. The wiring was totally shot. All the power was located in the main fuse box. The only way to get electricity to the other rooms was through the use of extension cords.

We did have water—in fact, some of the best water in the County. Soon after we bought the property, one of the members of our Bible Study Group loaned us the money to drill a well. The driller had to go down nearly four hundred feet before he found the aquifers he needed. He was boring through granite much of the time. The result was wonderful. We had sweet-tasting water while everyone else was drinking city water laced with chlorine.

I was reminded of the deep well on my grandfather's farm near **41**

Angola, Indiana. A tall windmill pumped water into a nearby horse tank. You could always get a cool, refreshing drink by taking the battered tin cup hanging on a baling wire hook at the pump, and holding it under the pipe to the tank.

After a year of restless waiting, we finally found a buyer for our Vienna home. During that period, more than a hundred people had traipsed through the premises. Some were just "looking" and comparing prices. Others were "bottom fishing."

Keeping a home on the market, month after month, is a homemaker's nightmare. The house must be kept picked up and spotless at all times since you never know when a prospective buyer will be knocking on your door. You can specify "By Appointment Only," but then you may ward off some potential buyer who is driving through your neighborhood. The scenario is similar to living in the display window of a downtown department store.

The couple who eventually bought our home are nice folks— Church of Christ people from the western states. They did not haggle over the price (which we had already dropped several times). They liked the house and appreciated its excellent condition. We were sorry to see it go, but we also knew that we had no other choice if the Center was to survive.

Although we had been moving piecemeal to Coral Road for over a year, we were now facing a deadline to get out of the house. One of the last items to be moved was my library that I had accumulated over years of preaching. I wanted to keep it intact as long as possible since I used it daily.

Even though we stepped up the moving momentum (plus practicing the ancient art of "pitch and throw"), it still looked as though we were going to miss our deadline. Then we received word that Lois's mom had died. The funeral was scheduled the same week we were to vacate the house. We needed help. Some of the young people from our church came by to assist us. One of these dear souls, Jim Sheldon, helped me move my bookcases. Books are heavy . . . heavy . . . heavy! By sunrise, we could hardly walk.

Finally, we were ready to leave for Illinois. The only way for us to arrive in time for the funeral was to drive all night. We were there the next morning, just two hours before the music started. Coming home, we were sobered by the thought that now, with all our parents gone, we were the older generation.

We returned from Illinois to take up "temporary residence" in the Old House at Coral Road. We assumed that our stay would probably be about six months—certainly no longer than a year. Lois called our new experience "camping out." We were hearing growing rumors that the commercial real estate market was beginning to make a comeback. Had we known that six months would become *six years*, we would have been swept away.

Once again, we debated the wisdom of remodeling the Old House, since the basic structure was sound. We reached the same conclusion as before. We could not justify spending between twenty and thirty thousand dollars, knowing full well that the house was destined for the bulldozers.

Our biggest problem at Coral Road was keeping warm in the winter. Houses built in 1904 were not insulated. Neither the garage nor the house had any heat. Virginia has the reputation for mild winters, but during the years we were staying at Coral Road, that reputation vanished. The thermometer was recording some of the lowest temperatures in a century.

We were able to cope using kerosene heaters, electric space heaters, electric blankets, and heating pads. But whenever the chill factor was ten degrees below zero accompanied by a strong west wind, we were cold. Our meager heating arrangement could not keep pace. During the "Storm of the Century" in March of '93, Lois was stranded at Andrew's for three days. I tried to keep warm at Coral Road by staying in bed under the electric blanket.

F-County keeps a computerized list of "derelict" houses. They send out inspectors periodically to make sure that no one is living in them. Again, we were facing the prospects of being evicted from our own property. During blizzards, the negative impact of the cold was offset by the positive knowledge that the official white trucks of the County could not make it through the snowdrifts blocking the driveway.

Although the Old House was primitive, it was still better than being out on the street. The thoughts of being thrown out again were **43** more than we could bear. Meanwhile, we were being ripped off by thieves. The previous summer, my rototiller was parked in the garden. A thief came in the night, carted off the five-horsepower Briggs and Stratton engine, and then tossed the frame in a nearby creek. Andrew lost painting equipment worth thousands of dollars.

I began to think about ways we could circumvent the County machine legally. So I decided to pay a visit to the chief inspector on the Herndon Police Force. I explained to him the problem we were having with theft on our property. I asked him if he had any problem with our securing a watchman to look after everything. He said that that arrangement would be perfectly legal. I thanked him for his help and wrote him a letter, confirming his decision.

Lois and I now became the guardians for Coral Road. I kept a copy of my letter to the Inspector near our bed. Now if a police car drove up our driveway in the wee hours of the night (usually they were after drug dealers), we had a letter authorizing our presence there.

We felt now that our youthful experiences during the Great Depression helped us deal with the physical difficulties we were facing. We were accustomed to waking up with ice in the drinking glass beside our bed. We often had no indoor plumbing. Water came from a well with a hand pump outside and a pitcher pump inside to the cistern. We huddled around a hard coal burner to keep warm in the winter. The bathroom was a "three holer" with a Sears and Roebuck catalog.

Once we had a handle on the problem of being evicted again, I think we could have managed the physical difficulties. The real problem was the mental and emotional strain. Our dealings with banks and, later on, a crushing tax burden put us under a heavy weight. Some unrelenting personal critics who were second-guessing all our moves compounded our painful struggle.

2. Farming the Farmers

When I was a student in seminary, a kindly old professor said to us in class one day, "Boys, when you get out on the field, one of the first things to do is to make friends with the local banker. After you get moved into the parsonage and the local papers have announced your arrival, put on your best suit and go downtown to meet with the bank president. When you are in his office, shake his hand firmly and look him squarely in the eye. Before you leave, tell him that you want to borrow five hundred dollars for a year. Keep the money safe and pay it back in six months."

I followed the advice of my professor to the letter. After I began preaching for a rural church in Illinois, I drove over to our bank and did exactly as he said. I borrowed five hundred dollars and paid it back in six months. From that point on, I never had any difficulty getting a loan.

For many years, I drove Chevrolets and traded every two years. When I bought a new car, I called our bank president and told him how much money I needed. He always came through for me.

These were the days before computers were programmed to wring every last red cent from the customer. We had no monthly banking fees, no charge for every check deposited, no additional charge if the check originated from out of state, no charge for every check written, and money deposited on Friday evening counted from the time it was deposited, not three days later while the bank purloined the interest.

One of the farmers in our community bought a combine. Thinking that he had enough money to cover the cost of a new implement, he overdrew his account by forty thousand dollars. When the check made out to the dealership surfaced at the bank, one of the clerks was horrified. Rushing into the president's office waving the check in his hand, he asked excitedly, "What shall I do with it?" The president said calmly, "Honor it. He's good for it."

Banking was personal. People knew each other. They knew who could be counted on to pay. Balance sheets were beside the point. If the bank directors recognized that someone was honest, sooner or later they would get their money. It just might take a while. If you were having difficulties making payments, you could always talk to someone in the bank who had the power to help you.

When we moved to Washington in the seventies, our banking situation was similar to Illinois. Although the local banks were much larger, you could still get an appointment with the president or a vice-president, sit down, and look him in the eye. Many of the local banks in Washington had been operating for a century or more. A number of their employees had never worked anyplace else.

During the years that we have lived along the Atlantic Seaboard, we have watched the small banks being gobbled up by the conglomerates. When your bank goes into a merger, the chances are that you will lose all your friends there. Now your financial fate is in the hands of total strangers.

Our mortgage on Coral Road was with the same bank that had carried the financing for our Vienna house. We had dealt with them for eighteen years. We knew the president and several vice-presidents personally. We also had a friendly connection through our attorney, who knew some of the board members. We had a comfortable relationship with each other.

Local bank leaders understood what happened to many businesses after the Crash. In our case, they realized that two acres of land in a prime location were not going to pack up in the middle of the night and leave town. We continued to make our mortgage payments and they felt secure.

Then our relaxed banking situation changed overnight. We received an announcement through the mail that our bank was being bought out by a conglomerate. I will refer to them as C-Bank. We lost all of our personal banking friends. They did not "know us from Adam."

Now we began to be pelted with calls for financial statements. Whatever documentation we sent them, it was never enough. They wanted more information and they needed it yesterday! Furthermore, they needed a new appraisal.

We knew about the appraisal scam from former encounters. Many banks only work with appraisers who they know are in their pocket. If an appraiser keeps turning in high appraisals ("high" from the bank's point of view), then he or she is dropped from the approved list. The appraiser becomes the bank's "hired gun." It is all a game, but a deadly one, if you are the target.

We knew qualified appraisers who were recommended by our attorney. Each one was experienced and had the highest credentials.

C-Bank would have none of it. We were not surprised since we already knew how our owl was being boiled.

Coral Road in May had a certain ambience, especially if you stayed outdoors. Graceful, waving trees shielded the long lane. The five huge oaks in the front yard were just coming into their summer glory. Lilacs and daffodils bloomed in the back yard, along with wildflowers everywhere. And now, after years of toil and sweat, the lawn was a lush carpet of green. The setting was pleasant and restful.

The C-Bank appraiser came on a rainy day in March. The west wind was blowing a gale. It was cold. The trees were barren and the grass was brown. Snow was still on the ground. The Old House looked like a ghost ship on a wintry sea. We had no way of actually knowing whether these circumstances had anything to do with the amount of the appraisal. Someone has quipped, "Never tangle with a judge who has missed his breakfast or just had a fight with his wife."

Andrew and I met with the appraiser at Coral Road on that sullen March day. By now, Andrew had his own real estate license. He pointed out the extra value of Coral Road because it was a "spike" driven deeply into the thirty-five acres being developed around us. Coral Road had the benefit of the three most important words in real estate jargon—"Location, Location, Location."

The appraiser turned a deaf ear to everything we said. It was obvious to us that he had already made up his mind. Coming out to see our property was merely a formality. He stayed a little while and then disappeared through the gate. As we watched his taillights fade away in the mist and the rain down our long driveway, a foreboding swept over me. I tried to sleep that night, but the night hags would not stop riding.

By now, the real estate market was beginning to come back. We did not expect our appraisal to come in at a million dollars, or even nine hundred and ninety thousand dollars, even though we had signed contracts for both these figures in our files. We knew that the rawness of the day should make no difference to an impartial appraiser. But since human beings are human, we discounted another fifty to seventy thousand on the weather score.

What happened next knocked us off our feet. The appraiser **47** turned in a final figure of *one hundred and twenty thousand dollars*. We were stunned! As the last straw, five thousand dollars was being billed to our account to cover the cost of *their* appraisal. Someone said that is like buying the bullet for your own assassination—in our case, because of the cost, we called it a "silver bullet."

C-Bank now held a gun to our head. Since our loan with them (according to their estimate) now exceeded the amount of collateral offered by Coral Road, they could foreclose at any time. If we could not pay, they could auction off our property on the steps of the F-County Courthouse. If the bid they received did not cover the cost of the mortgage, then we still had to pay the difference. We were facing a cruel situation.

During this period of time, I began doing some further research on banks. During the Great Depression, according to William Manchester, "In Cheyenne County, Nebraska, the leaders of two hundred thousand debt-ridden farmers announced that if they did not get help from the legislature they would converge on the state house and raze it, brick by brick." Foreclosure sales were thwarted by local citizens who bid ridiculously low prices and then turned the property back to the owner.

Since the reputation of bankers was so low, thieves were widely regarded as Robin Hoods. Local citizens protected John Dillinger and his gang, believing that he was handing out to banks their just deserts. An Indianapolis admirer wrote, "Dillinger does not rob poor people. He robs those who become rich by robbing poor people."

One farm editor wrote, "There are three great crops raised in Nebraska. One is a crop of corn, one a crop of freight rates, and one a crop of interest. One is produced by the farmers who by sweat and toil farm the land. The other two are produced by men who sit in their offices and behind their bank counters and *farm the farmers*."

3. "When Crying, Stung By Bee In the Face"

The Japanese equivalent of "It never rains but it pours," is "When crying, stung by bee in the face." We were about to get stung hard. We were still reeling from the blow left by the appraisal of $120,000 by the accomplices of C-Bank when we received a notice from F-County that the Center owed $70,344.49 in taxes. Furthermore, it was due now.

The bill might as well have been seven hundred thousand dollars or seven million. We did not have it. We were biting our fingernails each month just to get the mortgages paid. So far we had managed to keep up, but now it looked like the end.

The distinguished Virginia justice John Marshall wrote, "The power to tax is the power to destroy." F-County had been huffing and puffing for several years. Now they were about to blow our house down.

Early on, our attorney had been informed that since the National Church Growth Research Center is a not-for-profit missionary organization, we were exempt from real estate taxes. We had a similar situation in Illinois where the Center owned a staff house, but we did not pay taxes on the property. Now the bureaucrats in Virginia changed their minds. They said we had to pay.

And what was their appraisal for tax purposes? A figure jumped out at us from a letter we received from the County that made us laugh and cry at the same time. Their assessment was based on an appraisal of $407,040.

How interesting we thought. C-Bank had just assured us that their appraisals are done scientifically. All guesswork is eliminated. Their evaluations were done by professionals who "knew their business." But now we had another appraisal that was nearly four hundred percent higher. We were assured by the County officials, "Our appraisals are done scientifically by professionals who know their business." It did not take a great deal of insight to know that something was rotten in the state of Denmark.

We tried to work out a deal. If the Bank would honor the County appraisal, we had more than enough collateral to handle our loan. If the County agreed to the Bank appraisal, we could probably squeak by on the taxes. Neither side was listening. All we said was just so much noise in a can.

Now we were caught, as a friend put it, "Between two seven hundred pound gorillas." On the one hand, we were dealing with one of the richest banks in the country. On the other, F-County is one of the wealthiest counties in America. We thought about that poor beggar at the gate of Dives who only wanted a few crumbs from the master's table, but who received nothing.

Our situation had looked hopeless because C-Bank was threatening to foreclose. Now it looked tragically hopeless. Between the Bank and the County, we were dead meat. All that remained was to see how they were gong to carve up the carcass based on their "scientific appraisals."

F-County had already evicted our Bible Study Group from Coral Road. Now, to add insult to injury, they were taxing us out the wazoo on land where we were being denied full ownership usage. Isaiah rails against the rich and powerful in his day who "turn aside the needy from justice" and "rob the poor of my people of their right" (10:2). Those citizens must have felt that they were also stung in the face by a bee.

4. Slings and Arrows

Lois and I are no strangers to criticism. Early in our ministry, we were involved in the relocation of a country church that had worshipped in one spot for over a century. Old habits die hard. We took reams of reproof for our participation in building a new house of worship in a more central location.

During the years that I served on the Executive Committee of Key 73, an effort in American cooperative evangelism that involved more than one hundred religious groups and organizations, I received letter after letter, castigating me for "selling out the Restoration Movement."

I remember one day seeing Dr. James Deforest Murch sitting in the lobby of the Sheraton Jefferson Hotel in St. Louis. I approached him with this question: "Dr. Murch, when almost everyone else in our Brotherhood was preaching isolationism, you were actively participating with a number of religious groups. How do you explain your response?" "Oh," he said, "I just took one of our early mottos—'we are not the only Christians but Christians only'—and went from there."

When I accepted an invitation to speak for one of the early Illinois state conventions, I received a caustic letter from one minister telling me that I should stay in Washington because I had "left the Faith." I sent him a copy of *Christian Growth* to let him know that I may not be as far out as he thought I was.

Someone has said that Americans should build the triumphal arches to their heroes out of loose bricks. Then later on, after the public turns against them, they can pull out the bricks and hurl them at their former champions.

Our previous experience with disapproval did not really prepare us for what was coming. My dad used to say that the most sensitive nerve in the human body goes directly from the spinal cord to the billfold in the left hip pocket.

In order to swing the purchase of the Methodist Church, it was necessary to borrow from individuals for the down payment. We planned to pay them back with monies from the sale of Coral Road. Then the real estate crash came, leaving us with two huge mortgages. We wrote to our lenders and tried to explain as fully as we could what our situation was. We assured them that their investment was safe and asked for additional time.

The majority of lenders were gracious and understanding. Some said they were forgiving their loan and making it a tax-deductible contribution. Some wrote kind letters and told us they were remembering the Center in their daily prayers.

Others were impervious. They treated the Center like a child that was misbehaving. They would supply the scolding and the rod. Some letters were hard-hearted; others were downright cruel. They did not want any explanations. We began to have a better understanding why Christian churches are known in religious circles as "The Brotherhood that shoots its wounded."

We were now locked into mortgage payments of nine thousand dollars every month. By renting out space in our church to other religious groups, we were able to help alleviate the strain. At one point, a Latino church, a Chinese church, and an African-American church were all meeting in our building. Their combined attendance was over six hundred worshippers. Every Sunday, our parking lot was filled to capacity. Even the lawn was covered with vehicles.

On the other hand, although the rentals on our building helped to keep the wolf away from the door, we were hit with higher utility bills. Sometimes, I would go over to the church in the wee hours of the morning and find the place lit up like a Christmas tree. The last group out had left all the lights burning with the thermostat set on ninety. Also, our maintenance bills were excessive since our building was being subjected to so much wear and tear.

When someone wrote and said that they wanted their loan repaid "now," we usually responded by saying that if we paid them, we would have to miss a mortgage payment. If we did not keep up with the banks, they would foreclose and take everything. By losing our collateral, others would be out in the cold. This thought did not seem to bother certain people. "Business is business," they retorted.

Ironically, it was usually the people who had the most money who wanted to push us to the wall. One dear friend, an elder in a Virginia church, had loaned the Center a thousand dollars. He told me on the phone that if anything happened to him, the money would become a gift. Unfortunately, I did not get his promise in writing.

When he died suddenly, his wealthy son-in-law wrote and said that he wanted the note repaid with interest. When I called him and told him what his father-in-law had said, he would have none of it. He told me he would file a lawsuit.

After we paid the note and the interest, several others informed us that the deceased elder had confided in them that he planned to forgive our loan. They said they would be willing to testify. But by then it was too late.

At the time we were living in the Old House, an irate farmer accused us of living "in the lap of luxury in a large Victorian mansion." When we showed his letter to some of our friends, they laughed. Better send him a picture of your "Victorian mansion," they said.

Another lady wrote, "If your father were alive, I know how ashamed he would be of you." Just how she became privy to that piece of information, I was not sure. Since I knew my dad better than she, I think he would have applauded our efforts to hang on in the midst of such difficulties.

After a while, it seemed that we could not win for losing. Some of our critics said that we were not doing enough to communicate with people. Others wrote and accused us of wasting too much money on postage.

Someone has said that humor is the shortest distance between two people. It really hurt us to find out that a few of the friends we had known and loved through the years had turned against us. It is sad to pick up the phone and talk with someone with whom you once had shared laughter, only to receive a cold and formal response on the other end. Many times, the rumors that they had digested were a series of inaccuracies, but they had swallowed them "hook, line, and sinker."

One of the rumors flying around said that we had been involved in real estate speculation. "We had many offers on Coral Road," they said, "and we had turned them down." The truth is, we had a number of "feelers" (some were bottom fishing), but only two contracts with earnest money. We signed both of them.

The people who did us the most damage were not those who shot us personally with their "slings and arrows." These missiles always stung, of course, and they usually came when we had just received another major blow from the Banks and/or the County. When some of our critics went to their church mission committee and tried to get us knocked out of the church budget, their actions really hurt the Center and The Safety Net program.

I am reminded of the practice that was prevalent in England and America during much of the nineteenth century—debtors were sent to prison. London's infamous Newgate Prison held a host of inmates who were indigent. While the father was incarcerated, many times his wife and children would be starving.

John Howard Payne was an American in England operating a theatrical company. He penned the words to that classic song, "Home, Sweet Home." When his theatrical company failed, he was jailed for debt. Lois and I have often thought about his plight, especially when we visited his grave in a Georgetown cemetery in Washington.

After he was released from prison, Payne, still penniless, remarked how ironic it was to walk down the streets of a strange city and hear the strains of "Home, Sweet Home" coming from a nearby cafe when he had no place to stay.

Finally, someone "awoke and smelled the coffee." If you jail a man for debt and thus deprive him of a chance to make his livelihood, how will he ever be able to pay his creditors? Furthermore, what about a humanitarian concern for his wife and children?

We could never figure out what the people who lobbied to get us taken out of the church mission budget had to gain. We were almost drowning the way it was. If they insisted on cutting the lifeline that kept us from drifting out to sea, how would they ever get their money? What they were doing did not make a great deal of sense.

Many Americans honor no code but success. If a football player kicks the winning field goal in an overtime game, he is heralded and feted. On the other hand, if he misses, even by three inches, he may get sacked. We have little room in our system for failure. If a person is having trouble, then it is somehow his fault. Therefore, he should be punished.

5. The Gift Horse

One day when I was working in the office, a call came from a lady who said that she and her husband wanted to donate a mobile home to a church. Would we be interested? I assured her that we were. At the time, her offer seemed like manna from heaven.

I have already described our living conditions at Coral Road. The Old House was really never a home—only a place to park until we could afford another place to live. Lois has always enjoyed decorating the houses where we lived, but as far as she was concerned, the Coral Road house was hopeless.

The only problem we saw with the mobile home was its distance from Herndon. It was located an hour south of Washington, just off the busiest stretch of highway in America—I-95. On the other hand, we knew that thousands of people working in the metropolitan area commuted an hour each way every day. Some workers who lived in the Eastern Panhandle of West Virginia were traveling three hours daily.

When we saw the mobile home, we were ecstatic. The dimensions were fourteen by seventy-four. It had modern appliances. It had central air conditioning and a good furnace. It had ample space. When we were building our home in Lincoln, we lived in my sister's trailer that measured eight by thirty-eight. We called that dwelling a trailer. This place was definitely a mobile home.

If our negotiations fell apart with the Banks and the County, at least we had a place to land. Coral Road was not much, but it definitely beat having nothing. It gave us reassurance to know that we had a haven during a time of storm.

Lois began dressing up our new home almost immediately. She moved in some of our furniture that was stored in the Mail Room along with her special dishes. I did not realize until then how strong the nesting instinct is among women and how much a place of their own means to them.

Since the mobile home had not been occupied for a few years, it needed a thorough cleaning. After several weeks of elbow grease and cleansers, the whole place was sparkling. Now at last, we had a cozy place to call home. We did not even have to be ashamed to invite guests.

We decided to maintain a residence at Coral Road since that property was located close to our offices. On the other hand, we wanted to spend as much time as possible in our new corner of the world. We felt encouraged about our whole situation.

A week later, we drove down to our new home to meet Andrew, Martha, and Rachel. We wanted to show them why we were so excited about our new facilities. When we opened the door, a horrible stench assailed our nostrils. Both bedrooms were covered with wastewater from our neighbor's toilets. The water had soaked into the carpet and was discoloring the beautiful wood paneling.

We called the owners of the trailer park to try and find out what had happened. It seems that the problem with the sewerage backing up had occurred before. The trailer park owners had installed back-flow valves in every trailer to keep waste from overflowing from the toilets. In our case, however, we were skipped because no one lived there.

Since every other mobile home had a back-up valve, we not only had our own wastewater back, we also received the spillage from all the trailers up the hill. Emotionally, we felt that we could not handle one more blow. The red needle on our disaster gauge was already pegged. But we knew that we had to act quickly to save the floors. The whole dirty mess had to be cleaned up as quickly as possible.

We set a day to return, but by now I had the flu. Since it was the only opportunity to get away from the office, we went anyway. We brought a wet-dry vac with us along with more cleaning supplies. I was too sick to work for any length of time. Our first step was to scoop up the waste in a dustpan and put it in garbage bags. I never felt worse and the aroma did not help any.

We filled three large plastic bags with the kind of material that usually goes *down* the toilet instead of *up* the toilet. We lugged the bags to the back of our van and headed back to Coral Road.

We turned off I-66 and on to Fairfax County Parkway. When we reached the intersection at Route 50, the light turned red. It was rush hour and the traffic was heavy. Four cars and a small truck were between the light and us.

As we sat there waiting for the signal to turn green, we were musing about the events of the day when, *KAWOOM*, we were slammed by a BMW that struck the rear of our van. We were catapulted into the small pickup in front of us. The sudden impact broke both front seats and Lois and I were thrown on our backs. Five additional vehicles had been rear-ended.

People came staggering out of their vehicles, wondering what had happened. The abrupt jolt made our rear doors fly open and one of our bags of waste hit the windshield of the BMW. The other two bags were along the wayside. Soon the police cars and the ambulances were everywhere. The owner of the BMW had fallen asleep (a fact that he would later deny in court) and we were all paying for his snooze.

We loved our red van, and now to see it towed away with both ends mangled beyond repair was a sad spectacle. It started to rain. I had to cross a ravine in order to call Andrew. Meanwhile, a lady police officer was quizzing the passengers of each automobile to see how they were. When she came to Lois, she asked if the black bag on the windshield of the BMW was ours. Lois replied, "Yes it is [she paused], but he can have it." Then she explained briefly to the officer about our day and what was in the bag. She said sympathetically, "Oh, you poor people. You've had a terrible day."

When the tow truck brought our van to Coral Road, we hoped that the three bags had been left behind. Some thoughtful officer, it seems, realizing that the bags belonged to us, had dutifully stashed them back in the van. Then he or she had tied the two mangled rear doors together with a clothesline rope so they could not possibly escape again!

After our fiasco, we called the trailer park personnel and told them what happened. They assured us that their insurance company would take care of all repairs. They told us that we needed to get an estimate. It took several weeks before we could find a contractor who was interested enough in the job to give us a bid. When we heard from him, we found out that a conglomerate had bought out the insurance company with which we had been dealing. The new company informed us that they would not accept any responsibility for our mobile home.

Now we needed several thousand dollars for repairs (which we did not have) along with two hundred dollars each month in trailer park rent. Eventually, when we sold the mobile home, we would get our investment back. Meanwhile, our housing prospects were bleaker than ever.

I grew up in rural Indiana, where the saying was, "Don't look a gift horse in the mouth." Buyers tell the age of horses by looking at their teeth. But if someone *gives* you a horse, then this procedure is unnecessary. By now, we wish we had looked more carefully at our "trailer horse." Even then, we had no way of knowing the chain of events that would follow.

6. Long Dark Nights

The sale of our home in Vienna brought a temporary reprieve to the money problems for the Center. Even though we had sold at the bottom of the market, we cleared enough to ease the terrible financial burden the Center was facing. We hoped that by the time our house money ran out, the real estate market would come back and we could sell Coral Road. It was not to be.

Many churches and missionary organizations have reserve funds put away for emergency use. When a crisis looms, they meet the situation out of their own resources. Later on, they may try to replace these monies for the next difficult time. We did not have such a fund available, but we wished we did. When we were able to free ourselves from the present scrape, we decided to set up a Memorial Trust Fund for the future. If we had had the money, our situation could have been solved with the stroke of a pen.

By the time our Vienna house money began to dwindle, our nagging fears returned. What on earth were we going to do now? We could let the Banks and the County take everything and fight over the remaining bones. But where would that plan leave us? We would have to start all over again. On the other hand, without offices or a staff, how could we begin again?

A midwestern farmer called the Center, "a wild dream." One woman wrote: "Sometimes we just have to face the music. Why don't you just give up?" I cannot say those thoughts never crossed our minds. On the other hand, with the growing secularization of our nation, our goal, "Helping Churches Evangelize," took on added seriousness. We were feeling first hand the negative impact of pagans in power. With the addition of the Safety Net program, we were helping dozens of first-rate ministers find their way back to preaching again. With our country in a moral crisis, surely no mission is more crucial.

Another important factor in "staying the course" related to the good people who had loaned money for the down payment on the Methodist Church. With all our assets wiped out, how could they ever expect to get repaid for their kindness? We could not bear the thoughts of giving up when they had held up our hands with their prayers and their dollars.

If banking had not become so robotized, we could have gone to the president and explained our predicament. The chances are, he would have found a way to help us. But in Washington, we were dealing with faceless conglomerates run by hidden executives with soulless computers. Your fate could be sealed with a click of a mouse.

We were constantly dealing with lower echelon people in the banks who had no power to make decisions on their own. Every important resolution had to be referred to a "higher-up" who in turn had to submit everything to another "higher-up" and so on. We tried repeatedly to get the names of those who were deciding our destiny. Their subordinates had been instructed not to give us their names. The executives were all wearing hoods and they did not want to show their faces.

Meanwhile, F-County was stepping up their pressure on the taxes they were claiming. These were taxes from which we were supposed to be exempt as a non-profit charitable and religious organization. We decided that F-County has a two-pronged program of taxation: (1) Tax everything that is standing still; (2) Tax everything that moves. In the words of Percy Bysshe Shelly, we felt that we were under "the awful shadow of some unseen Power."

It was difficult for us to keep pushing down our fears—fears about disastrous consequences if we could not continue to hang on a little longer. It was F. Scott Fitzgerald, chronicler of the Jazz Age, who talked about the three-o'clock-in-the-morning fears being the worst of all. We knew instinctively that if we succumbed to our bogeys, they would sink us. We had to keep fighting off the demons of doubt or we would lose our will to soldier on.

Letters from our critics ran from ten sentences to ten pages. The lament was the same. You are not handling your finances properly. If you were, you would not be facing your current situation. We felt like some were saying, "We are predicting your failure and we want to make sure that our forecast comes true."

The church board of one supporting church debated our circumstances for an entire evening. Because they had experienced a similar financial crisis previously in their history, they had salted away six hundred thousand dollars in a Special Fund. Would they help us? No, they decided against it. Their reason (as reported by the missions chairperson), —it would be like "pouring sand down a rat hole." They could consider themselves fortunate, I would think, that **59** their supporters did not take a similar attitude toward them when they were going through their economic plight.

When you are being surrounded by constant gloom, even the slightest ray of sunshine brings encouragement. Through all our troubles, the mail carried the loving notes from people who to this day probably do not realize what their reassurance meant to us. These notes read: "Paul and Lois, we know that the Center is going through a severe financial struggle. We are so sorry. Here is an extra gift to help out this month. We wish it could be more. Meanwhile, we are lifting up your needs to the throne of grace every day." You never forget the people who help save your ship during a storm.

As I said earlier, Lois and I have never felt that we were immune to criticism— far from it. But many of the accusations we were receiving were off by light years. With all our efforts to communicate the truth of the situation, we could not believe how some people were so misinformed. Of course, we have dealt often with people who shoot from the hip. Now it seemed, their bullets were hitting the ceiling.

One church leader called me and harangued me about our "stupidity." We were inept. We were poor stewards of the Lord's money. We should never have moved to Washington in the first place, and on and on. I let him walk all over me for nearly two hours. When he finally took a breath and I had a chance to speak, the receiver clicked. In my mind's eye, I saw him following the example of the priest and the Levite, passing by on the other side when he saw a poor human being, naked and helpless, lying along the Jericho road.

Mark Twain found himself in financial trouble over a publishing venture. His board of directors advised him to declare bankruptcy. Instead, he wrote to his creditors and begged them for mercy and more time. Then he set out on a worldwide lecture tour. He sent his fees back to cover his liabilities. Finally, that glad day came when he had cleared his last debt. A friend asked the famous author how he had managed to survive. "Only one thing kept me going," he said, "the unalterable belief that this task was utterly impossible."

III.

The

Rescuers

There is a friend who sticks closer than a brother.

Proverbs

Man must be given a chance to manifest his gifts
in creative energy, he must not be overwhelmed
with external commands and have his life encumbered
with an endless number of norms and prohibitions.

Berdyaev

III. THE RESCUERS

1. Places in the Heart

By the fall of 93, our financial picture looked bleak indeed. We had downsized wherever we could. Our staff was just a skeleton of what it had been during the days of the Bicentennial Venture in Evangelism, The American Festival, and Congress 88. Lois and I were camping out at the Old House on Coral Road in order to conserve funds.

Once you cut away the meat, you are down to the bone. You cannot function without utilities, telephones, office equipment, repairs, and so on. In other words, your reductions can only go so far. Then if you continue cutting, you will injure or kill the patient.

From the beginning, the National Church Growth Research Center has been supported by its friends. Included with this group are a number of churches that put the Center in their mission budget. Their gifts range from ten dollars monthly to five hundred dollars. We refer to this group of selfless givers as "Partners."

Our friendship with many Partners of the Center goes back a long way. Perhaps Lois and I held an evangelistic crusade in their church. Some Partners were former students in my classes when I was a professor. (When you approach former students about missionary support, you always hope that you gave them an "A"!) Sometimes congregations using our evangelistic resources decided to show their appreciation and gratitude by including the Center in their mission budget. These Partners are more than just names on a computer list to us; they each have a place in our hearts.

With the Banks and the County constantly breathing down our necks, we had no other place to go except to these gentle and selfless people. After all, they were the ones who had launched the Center in the first place. They were the ones who had made possible the production of over five hundred evangelistic resources, including books, pamphlets, manuscripts, notebooks, audiocassettes, and more. They were the ones who had helped us coordinate two major Festivals of Evangelism. And they were the ones who were helping bruised and dejected ministers through the Safety Net program.

We decided to send out letters to those on our mailing list, telling people about our financial struggles. These letters were often three and four pages long. We felt it was impossible to explain our complicated circumstances in just a few paragraphs.

We knew at the time that we were running a risk by being so transparent about our state of affairs. The slightest scent of financial trouble sends some people scurrying over the side like mice abandoning a stricken vessel. We decided at this point to be as inclusive as possible and let the people themselves make up their minds. We had to take the risk of their jumping ship.

The chairperson of one mission committee said that they were dropping us until we got out of debt. That approach is analogous, I think, to the physician who says, "I can't do anything for you unless you are well," or the dentist who explains, "Come back and see me when your tooth stops hurting."

While Lois and I were ministering to a town and country church in Illinois, our congregation supported a missionary in India. Our gifts continued over the years. Then one day she wrote about a severe crisis they were facing. She needed financial help immediately.

When the leaders of our church learned about her situation, no one even suggested that we find another missionary to support. No one accused her of poor stewardship. No one asked for an updated financial statement. Instead, her plight was brought before our whole congregation. We took up a generous offering and wired her the money. I will never forget her letters of sincere gratitude.

For every individual or church that had their doubts about the Center, there were dozens of others who responded in a kind and large-hearted way. These people reacted to our tax emergency by sending thousands of dollars. Some churches took up special offerings. Others voted an extra gift from the mission's treasury.

We will never forget that wonderful day when Lois and Letitia drove to the huge government center for F-County and found the tax offices. Critics refer to this maze of towering buildings as the Taj Mahal because of its opulence. During the "crash" when thousands of businesses were going bankrupt, F-County was building its palatial headquarters of granite and marble. They symbolize the "gold-plated" government of F-County. Because of the generosity of our beautiful Partners, we were able to bring the checks that liquidated all our imposed taxes.

Our situation was comparable, we felt, to a boat that is caught in the rapids and is heading toward the falls and disaster. Some on the shore were pointing their fingers and shouting, "You shouldn't be out there in the first place." Others did not say anything. They just stood on the bank with their arms folded, watching our helpless craft rush by. Still others waded out into the turbulent waters as far as they could and threw us lifelines. Then they worked to pull us safely to shore.

The Apostle Paul ministered to many congregations, but only one (so far as we know) reached out to help him financially. That was the Philippian church. The warmest letter in the New Testament was written to those caring people who opened their hearts and their pocketbooks when Paul was languishing in a cold and dank Mamertine prison in Rome.

When he wrote to the Philippians, his soul was overflowing with gratitude. He said in response to their gifts, "I thank my God in all my remembrance of you, always in every prayer of mine for you all making my prayer with joy, thankful for your *partnership* in the gospel from the first day until now" (1:3-5).

As we read that passage over and over, we began to experience a fuller understanding of the depth of Paul's feelings. These early Christians were not just names on a church membership roll. Each person held a special place etched in the Apostle's heart.

2. The Third Gorilla

By the spring of 95 our financial tension had eased considerably. You will recall that our tax consultant told us that our banking situation with C-Bank and our tax debacle with F-County was like being caught between two seven-hundred-pound gorillas. Now both gorillas had been caged.

Our tax advisor had pursued our problem with the County all the way to the top tax official. When he refused to budge, our consultant said, "Well, Mr. G., you have appraised Coral Road for $402,020.00 and C-Bank has appraised the same property for $120,000.00. "This seems to me," he said, "to be the kind of story that a TV program like *Sixty Minutes* would like to pick up." In a few weeks, we learned that F-County had revised their estimate.

We were able to put the C-Bank gorilla to bed by finding a Christian lending institution. In this case, we had known the vice-president for more than forty years. After we explained what had happened, their board voted to loan us the money to pay off C-Bank. Now we had a fifteen-year mortgage and our payment reduced the principle by over a thousand dollars each month. We were breathing more easily and sleeping more soundly.

Then out of the urban jungle came gorilla number three. The name of this gorilla was N-Bank. C-Bank held the mortgage on Coral Road. We had paid them off! N-Bank held the twenty-five-year mortgage on our church building. But first, I think a word of background is important.

N-Bank was another conglomerate, new to the Washington area, that was gobbling up every small bank in sight. The hundred-year-old Washington Bank that held the twenty-five-year mortgage on our church building was one of their tasty morsels.

Once again, we were fearful about our financial matters being thrown into the laps of strangers, but this time we were fortunate. The senior vice-president who handled our account in the new bank merger was open and friendly. He had worked in financial institutions for many years.

Fred B. did his homework. He studied the history of the Center and the Coral Road property. He was not nervous about N-Bank getting their money back. He knew that in time, the real estate market would return and that we would settle our debt.

Fred was always accessible. If you had a problem, you could discuss it with him without being treated as though you were wasting his time. We even joked with each other. Our relationship was a comfortable and reassuring one.

Our twenty-five year mortgage was reviewable every five years. Our original bank had assured us when we signed the papers, that as long as we made our monthly mortgage payment, the five-year examination was more or less a formality.

Fred called me about two months in advance of our five-year review, and we began filling out the paperwork. Based on our annual income through the Center and the rent we were receiving on our church building, Fred thought that we merited a reduction in our current interest rate. We set up a date to sign the renewal papers.

Two days before we were to meet in Fred's office, we received a phone call that stunned us. Fred told us that he was being fired by N-Bank along with a number of other senior officials. Called the "chain saw approach," a corporation simply lops off its top executives and hires young employees to fill their slots.

The reasons for such drastic action are sordidly economical. The current senior officials have worked their way up the corporation ladder, and consequently, they are receiving the largest salaries and the most benefits. By getting rid of them, the company can hire cheaper help as replacements. The whole venture is a heartless one, designed mostly to keep the stock analysts on Wall Street happy. If workers trust a company and feel that their future is secure, the blow can be psychologically devastating.

Fred was replaced by a much younger official with a bean-counter mentality. Although we had already filled out all the forms necessary to renew our loan, the new official conjured up more hoops for us to jump through.

After responding to one questionnaire, we received yet another, and another. We wondered if he was going to put all this paper on a scale and judge us by the pound. As the days wore on, we became more restive.

A few days later, two good-looking young bank employees came to visit with us at the church. They wore trench coats and were impeccably dressed. They had only recently started their banking careers and were working their way up the corporation ladder.

The officials came by to inform us that N-Bank was not going to renew our mortgage. We asked them why we had been approved before and were being turned down now. They said that they could not answer that question. As the men turned to leave, I almost felt sorry for them. I thought about telling them that they were giving their lives to a faithless company that would cut them loose when they reached the ranks of senior management. I decided against saying anything since they would not believe me anyway. I would just be wasting my breath.

I went to bed that night but I greeted the dawn with sleepless eyes. The next day was one of the worst in my entire life. A chilling west wind kept me from ever getting warm. I sat in my reading chair, looking out the window in a kind of stupor, staring at the falling snow that was drifting down in huge flakes. I never even bothered to turn on the lights. Meanwhile, the "Terrible Ifs" Winston Churchill talks about were accumulating.

The two men from the bank told us that the decision not to extend our loan was final and irrevocable. I decided to go ahead anyway and write to the president of N-Bank who lived three states away. In my letter, I reminded him that we had always made our mortgage payments. Furthermore, if they foreclosed, not only would our church be out in the street but a Latino Church, a Chinese Church, and an African-American Church would be out there with us. I marked the envelope "Personal."

The bank president ignored my letter. I wrote a second letter. He ignored it also. The minister of the African-American Church is a close friend of a Virginia senator. He (the minister) offered to talk to him. He did. The Virginia senator wrote to the bank president, pleading our cause.

This time we received a response in a few days from one of the corporation vice presidents. She was incensed that we enlisted the help of a U.S. Senator. She wrote a four-page letter saying in essence, "We do not like you people and we want you out of our hair."

Her letter contained five or six points as to why they were taking action against us. Most of her points were skewed and the last one was an out-and-out fabrication. Fred B., our former N-Bank official, put his future career on the line and answered her point for point. The lady was not happy. Bank executives, for the most part, do not like to be contradicted. Like the ancient gods of Greece and Rome, they prefer to rule by fiat.

This head-on encounter, however, bought us some much needed time. N-Bank treated us like an old dog with a skunk. They decided to leave us alone—at least for a while. They were already taking flak from the National Association for the Advancement of Colored People for racial discrimination. Evidently, they did not want to think about any more negative reports in the news media. If we had not protested loudly, they would have squeezed us like a banana.

Eventually, N-Bank got back every dime we borrowed along with as many additional fees as they could conjure up. Without the help of an African-American minister, a U.S. Senator, a former banking official, and a good attorney, it is doubtful whether or not we could have survived.

When my professor told us to find a good banker when we moved to town, his advice was right for that era. Nowadays, by the time you locate a banker, he or she will soon be transferred to another branch in another state.

If I were back in the seminary classroom, I would hand out the same advice, but I would tell the students to get a good lawyer, especially if they are going to be preaching along the Eastern Seaboard of the United States.

We were fortunate. Early in the history of the Center, we found an astute attorney who became a good friend. If someone writes Norman H. a hot letter, they get a scalding one back. If a Banker or Bureaucrat thinks that your group is defenseless, they do not mind pouring it on. The fact that you have a good defender makes most officials a little more wary.

In the midst of our fracas with N-Bank, we received an irate letter from a lady in a northern state who was rankling on the Center rather severely. In one of her criticisms she said, "How much longer will you keep on beating a dead dog? You can't lick city hall." I wanted to write back and say, "Our dog may be wounded but he is not dead." Then I wanted to say, "As far as city hall is concerned, maybe we haven't licked them, but at least they are uncommonly quiet right now."

3. The Language of the Soul

Lois and I were fortunate. We had both grown up in musical families. Her father, in addition to his preaching, led the high school band in Clearmont and Ravenwood, Missouri, and the Municipal Band in Lehigh, Iowa. Lois's mother continued playing the piano until she was 89.

My father and mother were also talented in music. In the absence of a choir director, my father would take over the church choir until a replacement could be found. My mother earned part of her tuition at Bethany College by being a piano teacher. Music is an important part of my family heritage.

During the terrifying days at Coral Road, I found myself rediscovering the value of music. Sometimes called, "The Language of the Soul," I began to seek more and more comfort in its solace.

We were blessed to have a place called the "Clothes Closet" within easy walking distance from Coral Road. The site of a former lumberyard, it had been leased by several churches who turned it into a kind of Good Will store. It was a veritable treasure-trove of castoff clothing, used furniture, electrical appliances, tableware, typewriters, and computers, along with books and records.

Most of the records were vinyl and you could pick them up for a quarter each. Since many music buffs were switching to CDs, you often found an entire album of classical music for a dollar or less. The romantic ballads of World War II were also available, along with religious albums. Meanwhile, I had my own music collection that I had built up over the years.

As our economic situation worsened and the financial pressure began to intensify, I found that I could no longer listen to the music I had previously enjoyed. Tchaikovsky and Mozart had been among my favorite classical composers; but now, much of their music was too "alive with nervous vitality and dynamism." My troubled soul needed something more soothing.

When I was in high school, our band often played the music of John Philip Sousa. I knew by heart the trombone part to "The Washington Post" and "The Stars and Stripes Forever." In my distressed state, I also had to let these triumphant marches go.

I did find emotional release in the agonizing melancholy strains of "Pathetique" in Tchaikovsky's *Symphony No. 6 in B Minor*. And who could fail to be moved by the haunting melody of "Lachrymosa" from Mozart's *Requiem*? This musical genius died a pauper and was buried in a storm of wind and rain in an unmarked grave in the cemetery of St. Marx, Vienna. Ironically, both masterpieces were written just a few days before the composers' deaths.

I also found comfort in the yearning songs of World War II. Although Lois and I were in grade school at the time, the memories of that terrible conflict are still indelibly etched in our consciousness. We both grew up in small towns at a time when gold stars were going up in our neighbors' windows.

One day as I was listening to songs from that era our granddaughter, Rachel, dropped by my study. I explained to her the meaning behind some of the music she was hearing. I told her that in Britain and the coastal cities of the United States, a blackout was imposed at night to make it more difficult for enemy planes or ships to find their targets. Many vehicles had their headlights painted black with the exception of a small rectangular opening.

I told her that the terrible war situation did not keep people from singing songs of hope. One of those songs was "When the Lights Go On Again, All Over the World." Although the cities were dark, one day the bright lights would be turned on again. While people were being buffeted daily by forces outside their control, that reality did not cause them to dissolve into despair.

70   Rachel also wanted to know about the bluebirds and the white cliffs of Dover. I said that the Straits of Dover run between France and England at their closest point—just twenty-one miles apart. The high chalk cliffs on the British side are spectacular, rising majestically 300 feet from "the slate grey waters of the English Channel."

During World War II, the cliffs became a symbol of British resistance. The whole nation broke into song, "There'll Be Bluebirds Over, the White Cliffs of Dover, Tomorrow, Just You Wait and See." Millions sang the words of this beloved ballad with misty eyes, clinging to their hopes of better tomorrows. Looking back on two World Wars, one historian stated his amazement that such beautiful melodies could come out of such harrowing conflicts.

But the songs that soothed my troubled spirit the most were the communion songs I had sung since boyhood. During my early years, my father was the minister for all the rural Christian Churches in Steuben County, Indiana. I attended Sunday School and worship at Hamilton, Metz, North Scott, and South Scott. I thought I was being persecuted because I had to listen to the same sermon four times. Later on, when I began preaching, I thanked God that I could still remember some of my father's messages.

I could not keep from choking up when I heard such favorites as "Jesus, Keep Me Near the Cross," "Beneath the Cross of Jesus," "There Is a Green Hill Far Away," "O Love That Wilt Not Let Me Go," and "I Need Thee Every Hour." These songs were a part of my soul. They had an even deeper meaning for me because, in my mind's eye, I could see my father in the pulpit chair during communion, his head buried in his hands in a moment of solemn devotion.

As a boy growing up, how was I to know that these words and melodies would help sustain my sagging spirits during the worst experience of my life? I continued to praise God daily for parents who had provided me with a rich musical background.

I am fortunate to have a wife who shares the same appreciation for music. When our family first moved to Washington, Lois joined the Fairfax Choral Society, a widely recognized singing group in the Metropolitan Area. During the rehearsals, she became close friends with Doris and Nelva.

These talented ladies furnished the music in our church every **71**

Sunday morning. Their devotional songs at each worship service helped assuage my fears and restored a sense of calm to my storm-tossed heart.

4. A Place Called Ebenezer

Living at Coral Road was no "bowl of cherries," but the physical hardships paled into insignificance in light of the psychological and emotional torment. As John Dryden wrote:

> "Of all the tyrannies on human kind
> The worst is that which persecutes the mind."

Our greatest problem was trying to keep terror from building a home inside of us. We never knew when the corporate boot of the Bank was going to squash us like a bug. We were, after all, just an abstract entity, sealed away in the bowels of a huge computer. We were not flesh and blood human beings; we were just electronic charges on a hard drive.

I remember how much we cherished holidays, especially those that included a three-day weekend. We knew that during this period, the Banks and the County offices would be closed. Thanksgiving and Christmas holidays were even better. Then we could get a real break.

One day in late December, I called our attorney and told him how concerned I was that either the Bank or the County would take action against us. "Relax," he said, "all the Bankers and Bureaucrats are getting ready to take off for Christmas holidays. They are not even thinking about you." We loved him for his reassurance.

We also loved snowstorms. Washington is a southern city and a two-inch snowfall will practically shut the place down. With four to six inches of snow, life comes to a standstill. If the wind was blowing, the drifts piled up in our driveway so that no one could get in or out. We knew that our harriers were not ambitious enough to shovel the drifts and would therefore give us a few days respite.

Holidays and snowstorms offered us a few nights of sleep without the usual nightmares. We were trying to put into practice what Jesus taught—take life one day at a time. I had grown up with the

King James Version of Christ's teaching in the Sermon on the Mount: "Sufficient unto the day is the evil thereof" (Matt. 6:34). In other words, "You already have enough troubles for one day without thinking about what might happen tomorrow."

In the disciples' prayer (usually called the Lord's Prayer), Jesus instructed his followers to pray, "Give us this day our *daily* bread" (Matt. 6:11). The Master tells us that if we have our physical needs met for just 24 hours, we should not be anxious about tomorrow.

Although we tried to practice what Jesus taught, we discovered that if we kept our noses pressed too tightly against the mountain of our troubles, after a while, we could scarcely function physically or mentally.

Our coping powers had reached their limit. We had to get away from the office or go cuckoo. Frustrated, battle-weary, and exhausted, we found that if we could drop everything for a day, a half-day, or even a few hours, then we could muster up enough strength to come back to Coral Road and take up the burden again. Otherwise, we were gradually being driven to distraction.

When our daughter Letitia Jane came home from college, she and I would take a day off and ride the Metro into the District. Washington now has a beautiful and efficient rail system, one of the best in the world. The cars are clean and the stations are gracefully designed.

Letitia and I would board the Orange Line in Vienna, Virginia, our former home city. Since our first place to visit was Georgetown (and Georgetown has no station), we had to get off at Rosslyn and walk across the Potomac on Key Bridge. At the Rosslyn Station, you can experience a ride on what we have been told is the third longest escalator in the world (the longest is in Moscow).

Georgetown was a town long before the District of Columbia was established. At one time it was a thriving port city where the farmers from Virginia and Maryland traded tobacco and corn to the British. This exchange brought the colonists furniture, beautiful dishes, jewelry, and dresses, along with hundreds of other commodities.

We loved the bookstores in Georgetown. We also found a Canadian-owned hotel that serves hard English biscuits called **73** "scones." Letitia Jane usually ordered red raspberries with thick, rich cream. You can also have your choice of fragrant English teas.

The monument section of downtown Washington is delightful. Tourists by the hundreds of thousands come here each year. Standing on the steps of the Lincoln Memorial, you can look east toward the Capitol or west toward Arlington National Cemetery.

We often visited the Washington Monument. By taking the elevator to the top, you can get a breathtaking view of the entire city. When leaving, we would descend the 898 steps and review many of the 190 memorial stones on the way down.

In the original plan, the Washington Monument was supposed to be built in a straight line between the White House and the site of the Jefferson Memorial. When the engineers decided that the marshy ground would not support a heavy masonry structure, the monument was moved several hundred feet east. As a result, you are perfectly safe at the top. With the wind blowing thirty miles an hour, the 555-foot obelisk sways only one-eighth of an inch.

Enjoying these monuments and admiring the heroes they commemorate helped us realize that our struggles were small by comparison. On the other hand, being put out on the street is a bitter pill to swallow. So devastating is the impact of financial ruin, many American business leaders leaped to their death from hotel windows following the stock market crash in 1929.

We planned other escapes in the opposite direction from the Metropolitan Area. If Lois and I were getting away, we usually liked to head for the country. As William Cowper said, "God made the country and man made the town."

Virginia, Maryland, and Pennsylvania are the only places in the nation with "hunt country," based on the English tradition of fox hunting. Many of the farms are serenely beautiful. In addition to the luxurious manor house and the graceful stables (also air conditioned), you have the rolling fields and stone fences. Someone has pointed out that the millionaires live in Georgetown but the billionaires live near Middleburg, the heart of hunt country.

Our best time to get away was usually Sunday afternoon after

church services. We took along Geological Survey maps and followed the back country roads. Our journeys often took us to the confluence of the Potomac and Shenandoah Rivers at Harpers Ferry, the town that leaped into history after John Brown's raid. Thomas Jefferson wrote an article extolling this area as one of the great beauty spots of the world. He said, "The view was worth a trip across the Atlantic."

From Harpers Ferry, you can travel north into the Maryland countryside and see the large farm houses and the huge barns that were built by the German farmers who immigrated to this country several generations ago. In Prussia, they had been strangled by regulations. Petty officials were constantly in their faces. It must have been a wonderful joy to be able to breathe free air and work their own land without a bureaucrat lurking behind every bush and tree.

The little town of Brunswick on the Potomac was originally called New Berlin. But during World War I when Americans were shocked and outraged by German atrocities, the feelings against the "Huns" ran so high, the citizens of New Berlin found it necessary to change their name. During this chaotic time, American citizens stormed country schools and burned German textbooks. Ironically, the highway coming into Brunswick from Virginia is still named the New Berlin Turnpike.

Turning southwest from Harpers Ferry takes you deeper into West Virginia, the state where I was born. After crossing the Blue Ridge Mountains, you are now in the Alleghenies. These mountains are much higher and once you commit yourself to a road between the mountain ranges, you will probably be on it for miles. The whole atmosphere is so peaceful, you just want to keep on driving.

Since our struggle with the Banks and the County was so pervasive, it was difficult for Lois and me to move to other topics of conversation. On Sunday afternoons, we tried to declare a moratorium on any thought that was negative. I do not know the origin of the saying, "Think often of your friends, seldom of your enemies, and every day of Christ." Whoever said it provided us with a motto that is extremely helpful. Instead of letting our minds dwell on someone who had written us a stinging letter, we tried to concentrate on the beautiful people who shared our pain and were helping us shoulder the burden.

By traveling in the mountains, somehow we felt protected from an outside hostile world. We liked the charming little towns we passed through and enjoyed their unusual names: Rock Oak, Inkeman, Needmore, Bass, Lost City, Pansy, Brushy Run, Oak Flat, and Paw Paw. The breathtaking scenery all around us helped to bring solace to our troubled souls. We often saw a herd of deer drinking nervously from a nearby sparkling stream. When the leaves changed their colors in the fall, we enjoyed gorgeous vistas of yellows and reds and experienced "the overpowering beauty and sweetness" of a Virginia autumn.

When we watched cows grazing peacefully on the mountainside, with the clouds, white on blue, racing across the sky, we thought about our God who declared,

> "For every beast of the forest is mine,
> the cattle on a thousand hills."

We may be poor, but the God we worship "holds the whole world in his hands."

On our way home, we usually stopped by the Ebenezer Cemetery nestled in the foothills of the Blue Ridge Mountains. Ebenezer has an unusual history. Many confederate soldiers are buried here. Two former Baptist church buildings cover the knoll.

The "old" Baptist building was erected around 1755. Then a hundred years later, the Baptists got into a fight and one group split off and built a more imposing structure only a few yards away from the original house of worship.

Colonel John Mosby and his raiders (regarded as heroes by the South and renegades by the North) stopped a Baltimore and Ohio train. Among its passengers were U.S. Army paymasters who were carrying Federal payrolls. Mosby and his men divided $173,000 among themselves on the steps of the "old" Ebenezer Church.

In the southern part of the cemetery, we found a stone wall that was flat on top, about knee-high. The wall made a convenient place to sit while we wept and prayed. We tried to time our visit so we could watch the glory of the sun with its fading rays of red, orange, blue, and pinky-purple, as it slowly disappeared behind the Blue Ridge Mountains. We beseeched the Almighty for relief from our oppressive situation and the wisdom to deal with our oppressors.

One evening as we arrived, it had just started to sprinkle rain. We did not mind the soft drops falling on our faces. When we finished praying, a full moon was visible in all its brilliance. And behind us on the eastern horizon was a double rainbow. We remembered how God gave Noah the rainbow as a symbol of his promise. We believed that it was a good omen for our future.

We thought about the irony of finding refuge in a Confederate cemetery. When Lois, Letitia, and I came to Washington, we had just moved from *Lincoln*, Illinois. Furthermore, Lois is a distant relative of the Great Emancipator. She is a descendent of Abraham Lincoln's Hancock County cousins in Illinois. As her father, O. S. Lincoln, explained to her, his great-great-grandfather was Abraham Lincoln's grandfather's brother. But heartache makes us one, and here in a cemetery, a place of grieving, we did not think of North or South, but only of humanity and the endless struggles of human beings.

When we returned by nightfall to the long lane at Coral Road, it was with a sigh of sadness. Now we had come home to face our troubles for another week. Our brief respite had taken away our pain only momentarily. We realized that many battles lay ahead of us.

5. Precious Promises

Following his resurrection, Jesus met with his eleven disciples on a mountain in Galilee. Here he commanded them, "Go therefore and make disciples of all nations . . . ; lo, I am with you always, to the close of the age" (Matt. 28:19-20). Here is a promise, made not just for apostolic times, but also for all ages. Whenever we are involved in spreading the Gospel, we have the assurance that the Master will be by our side in a special way.

Sustained by his declaration, the early Christians set forth to conquer a pagan world. All the legions of imperial Rome could not halt these early believers from teaching and baptizing thousands. Finally, it was Rome itself that came crashing down.

The sequel to the resurrection is Christ alive forevermore. It was no fading memory that sustained these early disciples; it was the company of Jesus himself, dwelling in their lives through his Holy Spirit. Not only had he vowed his special presence while they were witnessing, he also promised his loving companionship when they were worshipping. "Where two or three are gathered in my name," he said, "there am I in the midst of them" (Matt. 18:20).

On the night of the Last Supper, Jesus told his followers, "I tell you I shall not drink again of this fruit of the vine until that day when I drink it new with you in my Father's kingdom" (Matt. 26:29). Over the centuries, whenever and wherever Christians have met to celebrate the Lord's Supper, Christ has been present in the midst of them, the silent and unseen Guest.

During the dark days at Coral Road, we came to rely on the precious promises of the Bible in an increasing way. We had no home, we had creditors and tax collectors hounding us, we had no money, we had former friends who had written us off; but above everything else, we still had the presence of the loving Christ and his pledge.

I have already mentioned the songs that we sang in an Indiana Sunday School and the way that the words and the music now took on new meaning for me. I also recalled my early Sunday School teachers and their Bible lessons.

The heroes of faith came back into my memory again and again. I thought about Noah—the townspeople thought he was crazy; Abraham—none of his friends could understand why he was packing up and leaving town; Moses—who gave up the riches of Egypt to become a nomad; Gideon—who vanquished ten thousand soldiers with his tiny band of three hundred; David—who stood before a towering Goliath with his sling and five smooth stones; Daniel—who prayed all night in a den of hungry lions. These Bible stories and others like them were burned into my consciousness.

For the believer, all the assurances in the Bible have merit, but they take on new luster and meaning when your back is up against the wall. We clung to Isaiah's reminder to a battered Judah and Jerusalem:

> But they who wait for the Lord
> shall renew their strength,
> they shall mount up with wings
> like eagles,

> they shall run and not be weary,
> they shall walk and not faint (40:31).

And again:

> When you pass through the waters
> I shall be with you;
> and through the rivers, they shall
> not overwhelm you (43:2).

The Psalms are also full of cheering promises. They have been a source of comfort to believers for centuries. Take for example, the one hundred and twenty-first Psalm:

> I lift up my eyes to the hills,
> From whence does my help come?
> My help comes from the Lord,
> who made heaven and earth (1-2).

Or again, the one hundred and twenty-sixth Psalm with its message of pledged fulfillment for those who labor in the harvest:

> He that goes forth weeping,
> bearing the seeds for sowing,
> shall come home with shouts of joy,
> bringing his sheaves with him (6).

Time and time again, I felt that our shabby home was illuminated by the presence of the living Christ. Samuel Rutherford, the Scottish Covenanter, was jailed for his religious convictions. He wrote to a friend from prison: "Christ came into my cell last night and every stone flashed like a ruby."

Sometimes, especially after a period of fervent prayer, he seemed so close, I could reach out and touch Him. E. Sinclair Hertel has written:

> Jesus shut within a book
> Is not worth another look.
> Jesus imprisoned in a creed
> Is a fruitless Lord, indeed.
> But Jesus in the hearts of men
> shows his tenderness again.

It is good to talk about the Jesus of Galilee and the Jordan, but we must also remember the Lord of the Chesapeake and the Potomac.

We kept praying for more wisdom. James says, "If any of you lacks wisdom, let him ask God, who gives to all men generously and without reproaching, *and it will be given him* (1:5). We constantly needed keen discernment.

As accurately as possible, we had to analyze what was taking place with the Banks and the County on a day-to-day basis. One misstep on our part and everything would be gone. It was also important to try and read the emotions of our opponents.

Andrew learned in his real estate classes that investment money flows plentifully into Virginia because the laws are slanted in favor of the lending institutions. Whereas the foreclosure process in some states can take months and sometimes a year, in Virginia, with the weight of the law in favor of the Banks, you may be evicted in a matter of days.

I agonized over every letter that I sent to the Banks and the County. If I rolled over and played dead (the response that Bankers and Bureaucrats like best), they would finish the job and bury us. On the other hand, if I were too aggressive, it would not take long for them to demonstrate who called the shots.

With each impending crisis I was forced to contact the Banks again. I found myself constantly asking God for help. Often when I went to bed, I could not sleep because I was mulling over another letter to an official. Sometimes the approach that seemed best came to me about three o'clock in the morning. I would get up and at least write out the gist of what I intended to say. Then I could go back to a more peaceful sleep.

Without the presence of Christ and the wisdom that comes from above, I have little doubt that our financial circumstances would have swept us over the falls to the rocks below. We would have been crushed. Our own mental processes would have been insufficient for the challenges we faced.

We could not have survived without the knowledge that the Lord was keeping his word to stay by our side. We kept harking back to

that wonderful promise in Hebrews:

"Never will I leave you;
never will I forsake you."

So we say with confidence,

"The Lord is my helper;
I will not be afraid.
What can man do to me?"
(13:5-6 NIV)

Paul and Lois Benjamin in Annapolis
beside the Chesapeake Bay

Old house and mailroom at Coral Road

Paul Benjamin,
baptizing in the Potomac River

The former Herndon United Methodist Church building

Mrs. A.P. Benjamin, minister's widow, attending a crab feast at Coral Road. After her husband died, she made her home with Paul and Lois Benjamin for 23 years.

"Twitty" — every missionary needs a cat!

Andrew, Martha, and Rachel Benjamin

Staff member, Letitia Jane Benjamin,
making Safety Net calls.

Washington, DC — Paul Benjamin in Ebenezer Cemetery (a Confederate Churchyard in the Blue Ridge Mountains) praying for release from the death-grip of the banks and county.

Two Baptist churches at Ebenezer Cemetery

IV.

In

Retrospect

Victory has a hundred fathers; defeat is an orphan.

An old military saying

The love of profits is always seeking
to overthrow the rule of justice.

Parrington

IV. IN RETROSPECT

I. Some Good Yesterdays

When Dr. Clovis G. Chappell, the world-renowned Methodist minister, came to Lincoln Christian Seminary to bring the Summer Lectureship on Preaching, he said, "Everybody needs some good yesterdays to stroll around in." Lois and I were fortunate. We had the remembrance of some good times in the past.

Our first congregation as ministers was the Prairie Green Church near Hoopeston, Illinois. Since that time, we have heard many horror stories about ministers and their first congregations. Our situation was different. Someone had taught these good folks to love their preachers. We felt warmed and accepted on every hand.

These folks are honest, sincere, hard-working rural people who major in showing kindness and compassion to others. When one of the farmers in our church had to go to the TB sanatorium, all the neighbors brought in their combines and harvested his crops. The ladies of the church prepared a delicious meal and carried it to the field so the men could keep on working.

During our summer revivals, the country roads were choked with dust from the dozens of cars that came from miles around. When our small church building could no longer accommodate the crowds, we moved to a huge tent. Finally, we voted to erect a new house of worship in the center of the township. Constructed with Bedford limestone, this building is one of the most beautiful in Illinois.

In addition to the revivals in our own church, Lois and I participated in dozens of evangelistic meetings from coast to coast. We spent one summer holding crusades throughout Africa. In Cape Town, the secret police attended our services every night to see if we were going to say anything critical about apartheid. In Ghana, we had street crowds of over five thousand. While I was preaching, I had to pause after each sentence to allow time for three interpreters.

One older evangelist used to talk about "barn-burning revivals." That phrase could be correctly applied to some of our crusades. During a two-week meeting, it was not uncommon to have seventy-five additions. Lois led a Crusade Choir each night to help with the congregational singing. She felt that she had learned a great deal from the Payne Sisters about the way to plan a song service. She tried to choose a moderate tempo that did not make the older people feel rushed or the younger people think she was leading a funeral march.

Lois talks about the "lilt"—that wonderful time when the instrumentalists, the choir, the congregation, and the song leader are all in synchronization. Listening to hundreds of people lifting up their voices in glorious praise to the Master is a high moment in Christian worship.

Our ministry changed dramatically after I accepted a teaching post in Lincoln Christian Seminary. By this time, I was deeply involved in a new cooperative evangelistic effort called Key 73. The name came from the Key Bridge in Washington, D.C., because the early planners held their first meetings at the nearby Key Bridge Marriott Hotel.

Key 73 gave me the opportunity to rub shoulders with some of the finest evangelistic leaders in the world. I became close friends with the Executive Director, Dr. Theodore Raedeke. Ted was a dyed-in-the-wool Missouri Synod Lutheran. He was also a great preacher.

I worked out an arrangement with President Hargrove at the Seminary that allowed me to teach all my classes on Mondays, Tuesdays, and Wednesdays. Then the rest of the week, Ted and I were on the road holding Key 73 Workshops all over the nation. Our **89** guidebook for each workshop was the two hundred and fifty page, *Key 73 Congregational Resource Book,* probably the most comprehensive publication on evangelism at that time. Together, we covered the major population centers.

During the years that we were traveling so extensively, Ted figured out one day that we had spoken to over 100,000 American ministers, a total of one out of every six ministers in America. Ted and I differed on many doctrinal issues. We had late-night discussions on the meaning and form of Christian baptism. But our hearts beat as one when we talked about people coming to Christ and living by the power of the Holy Spirit.

Ironically, it was Key 73 that helped launch the National Church Growth Research Center. Because I had made so many new friends through the Key 73 movement, when this campaign was over, speaking invitations kept coming. By this time, I was feeling the pressing need for more books and resources in the field of evangelism. Every other Christian field, it seemed, had a plethora of materials. You could buy many books on Christian Education, Counseling, Preaching, and Church History, but resources on Church Growth were sadly lacking.

To tell the complete story of the National Church Growth Research Center, at this point, would take us away from our main train of thought. All I can do from time to time is to garner a few highlights.

2. More Good Yesterdays

Partly because I had many acquaintances in national Christian circles, I was chosen to be the Executive Coordinator of a new evangelistic endeavor to be known as the American Festival of Evangelism. Key 73 did not have a national gathering. Instead, regional meetings were held across the nation.

By now, however, American leaders in evangelism wanted to follow up Key 73 with a major national event. They chose the National Church Growth Research Center to coordinate this new effort. The three years of preparation for the Festival were a major operation. The combined staff on the payroll in our Washington and Kansas City offices numbered over sixty, plus hundreds of volunteers. The budget was a million dollars.

Although we had offices in Tysons Corner, I did a great deal of my work out of my study in Vienna. It seemed that every time I went to the bathroom, the phone rang. Finally, I gave up and had a phone installed under the sink!

Although I received some flak from our own brotherhood for participating with the "denominations," for the most part, our churches were receptive to the idea. The delegation from Christian Churches in Kansas City was among the largest at the Festival. When the tallies were taken, the American Festival of Evangelism turned out to be the largest gathering of its kind in the history of North America. Over fifteen thousand participants were present at the closing night "Covenant Service."

Before I accepted the position of Executive Coordinator with the Festival, I called three of my older friends whose judgment I unreservedly respected. I called Carl Henry of Washington, D.C., Victor Nelson of Minneapolis, and Donald McGavran of Pasadena, California. They all gave me the kind of advice that comes only after many years in the trenches. Dr. McGavran told me that the Festival was not worth three years of my time and energy unless we preserved the materials.

Consequently, as soon as the Festival was over in Kansas City, we began the arduous task of getting written copies of all the presentations. If the speaker had a manuscript, then the process was fairly easy. If all he or she had was an audiotape, then we had to transcribe it and turn it into a manuscript. Since many of the speakers were world travelers, we tracked some of them down in London, Jerusalem, Cairo, and other parts of the globe. Robert Hart, William Palmer, and Philip Walter served as an editorial team along with the assistance of others.

We decided to gather the more than two hundred manuscripts into four *Reproducible Notebooks: Evangelizing, Discipling, Equipping,* and an introductory *Festival* volume. As I mentioned earlier, we voted to remove all copyrights so that a professor or Sunday School teacher could lift out pages and make additional copies for classroom work. Often during my Seminary teaching, I did not want to use a whole book but only brief sections. I was unable to photocopy the materials because of copyright laws. For this reason, the *Reproducible Notebooks* are a teacher's dream. I only wish that they had been available when I was in the classroom.

Because the Festival itself along with the *Notebooks* had made such an impact for Evangelism, some Christian leaders wanted another national gathering that included the major, mainline church bodies. The leadership of these churches, for the most part, had opted out of the Festival because Evangelicals had so heavily dominated it.

Congress 88, as it came to be known, met in Chicago, August 4-7, 1988. We had hoped to repeat the American Festival, but this time to be more inclusive. Many of the Evangelical leaders were strongly interested during the early stages of development. But later on, because they received such a backlash from the rock-ribbed Conservatives in their fellowship who accused them of being in bed with Liberals, they backed out. The situation was heartbreaking.

For years, Evangelicals tried to wean Liberals away from their all-encompassing social agenda. At this point, with their church membership figures sagging, the Liberals were willing to learn. Many of their own leaders said that their church had emphasized Matthew twenty-five to the exclusion of Matthew twenty-eight. They thought that a national gathering on evangelism could help remedy this need. But, alas, as it does so often, prejudice ruled the day. The Liberals opted out of bringing their membership to Kansas City; the Evangelicals opted out of bring their membership to Chicago.

Although the Presidents of the Evangelical bodies were afraid to publicize Congress 88 to their constituents, many came quietly, accompanied by their Director of Evangelism and other key leaders. At the same time, a number of Presidents from the so-called liberal bodies were there.

Because we have grown so numbers-conscious, we often fail to examine the weight of our figures. Bringing over four thousand church executives to Chicago may have had a greater impact on evangelism than the fifteen thousand ministers and "lay" leaders who attended in Kansas City. Although we did not try to repeat the Festival *Notebooks*, the audiotapes that resulted from the Congress were made available everywhere.

3. The Washington Roundtable

For many years, I sensed that one of the key players in Church Growth was the denominational Director of Evangelism. Almost every church body with an ecclesiastical structure above the local church has someone who fills this post. The importance of the position usually varies with the agenda of the President or chief officer. In the case of the Assemblies of God, the Director of Evangelism held a vital position because the General Superintendent, Dr. Thomas A. Zimmerman, was *pure* evangelism.

Because I had worked in Cooperative Evangelism for so long, I was on a first-name basis with most of the Directors of Evangelism in America. I liked them. Many of these fine Christian leaders were making huge personal sacrifices.

Since these Directors had no forum of their own (Professors of Evangelism had formed the Academy for Evangelism in Theological Education), we thought that it would be a good idea to bring them together for an annual gathering. For many of these much-traveled Directors, the only dates they had free were the holidays between Christmas and New Year's.

We emphasized the idea of a Roundtable to maximize the concept of equal footing. We had no C.E.O.s—just brothers and sisters in the Lord who wanted to see the Great Commission fulfilled.

These stalwarts in evangelism did not want to come together for more long speeches. Most presentations at the Roundtable were limited to fifteen minutes or less. It was a "hands on" kind of meeting. Every year, several Directors were selected to talk about what their group was doing in outreach. They brought along copies of the resources they were utilizing to help launch and sustain an effective program in Church Growth. We kept a strong emphasis on planting new churches. **93**

Before the Roundtable, most groups had been developing their own materials in the field of evangelism. Much of what they were doing duplicated what someone else had already done. We called this unnecessary overlap, "reinventing the wheel." Many Directors of Evangelism gained the permission from their superiors to follow the example of the American Festival and do away with all copyrights. In this way, every religious body could reprint evangelistic materials and beam it to their own constituents.

The Roundtable became one of the highlights of our year. Bringing these Directors together on an annual basis was like a family reunion. The potential influence of this group was incalculable. Although they numbered around one hundred or less, together they represented over one hundred million American Church Members.

Nothing we had ever started and had to let go saddened us like saying farewell to the Roundtable. Lois, along with the musicians from our church, Doris and Nelva, provided the music. Since it was the Christmas season, they always devoted one evening to carols. Listening to the deep and rich voices of these Directors as they sang with meaning, "O Little Town of Bethlehem," "O Come All Ye Faithful," and "It Came Upon a Midnight Clear" was a sweet and soulful experience.

After a decade of leading and facilitating the Roundtable, we were now too busy fighting Banks and Bureaucrats to carry on the work any longer. Each Roundtable took a tremendous amount of preparation and we simply did not have the extra time or energy. The Roundtable had become "A Bridge Too Far."

The Center now was in a survival mode where we wondered from one day to the next how long we could hold on. We needed to stay in close touch with our Partners and keep them abreast of our situation. This task was not an easy one because our state of affairs was in constant flux. We soon realized that what we said today might not be true tomorrow. Consequently, our critics accused us of discrepancies in our stories. We felt that our efforts were like describing a storm at sea. Those who had never been in our boat would find it impossible to comprehend.

In addition to our regular support, we needed to raise thousands of dollars to cover the taxes that were choking us to death. I did not want to give up my writing because, after all, developing new evangelistic resources was one of the major reasons why we had moved to Washington in the first place.

I also became vitally interested in the way that leaders survived in a crisis. What did Washington do at Valley Forge when the cause of American independence hung by a thread and the Tories kept chanting, "Give it up, George"? How did Lincoln cope with his daily trials, which included so many inept generals and a Congress that was critical of his leadership? As I have mentioned earlier, the heroes of the Bible and the way they triumphed over trouble occupied much of my attention. During our years at Coral Road, I was able to gather over six thousand notes to assist me in future literary endeavors.

For a long time, we wanted to do something more concrete to help stem the tide of ministers who were opting out of the pulpit. I had dedicated fifteen years of my life to the classroom in educating new ministers. Now something needed to be done to help those on the field who were hurting and discouraged.

Our own efforts to assist preachers were aided by a special grant that had to be supplemented from our mission funds. Today, this program is known as *Safety Net*. Hundreds of ministers and their families continue to be helped during a time of special need. The Safety Net Representatives contribute hundreds of dollars to this effort and provide human resources for guidance and counseling.

We were saddened when some of our former friends who had been by our side during our "successes," now began to grow distant. They simply ignored any of our efforts to get in contact with them. I recalled what that crusty old Prussian, von Rundstedt, told General Rommel when the latter took over the oversight of the Atlantic Wall. "Remember," he said, "victory has a hundred fathers; defeat is an orphan."

4. The Valley of Humiliation

As I look back now on our struggles at Coral Road, I have tried to come up with a single word that most aptly describes my feelings.

One word transcends all others—"humiliation." This term embodies the concept "to make low," "to humble," and "to abase." I felt each of these meanings in my bones.

Another word closely associated with "humiliation" is "mortified." This expression has as its root the thought of "death" or "being killed." It is the term from which we derive "mortician" and "mortuary." "Mortified" can also carry with it the idea of "embarrassment" or "being ashamed."

It was embarrassing to me that after so many years of marriage, I could not even provide a decent place for my family to live. I am aware of the text in First Timothy, "If anyone does not provide for his relatives, and especially his own family, he has disowned the faith and is worse than an unbeliever" (4:8). I had grown up with the King James Version: "and is worse than an infidel." Frustrated life insurance agents would sometimes quote the AV of this text to my father-in-law when he refused to take out their policy. Their tactic never sold him; it only made him angry.

Over the years, Lois and I have entertained hundreds of visitors in our home. When we lived on the campus of Lincoln Christian College, our five-bedroom residence was the unofficial guesthouse for the school. When company came, we felt that we received more than we gave. But now, with no suitable place of our own, the entertaining had stopped.

When Letitia Jane brought her college friends to Washington over the holidays, she wanted to bring them by the Old House at Coral Road. We said, "No." She was baffled by our response. She said, "Oh, they will understand. Many of them come from families that don't have much." We still said, "No." We were too embarrassed by our circumstances to have anyone visit.

Lois has always loved to cook, but now she had no kitchen. She did most of her meal preparation at the home of our daughter-in-law. I began to realize that to deprive a homemaker of her kitchen is like taking away the library from a writer.

In addition to cooking, Lois also enjoys flowers. She has a green thumb and soon after we moved into a new place, she was busy planning her flower garden. She planted annuals—pansies, geraniums, and her favorite, rosebud impatiens. She also had perennials—phlox, coreopsis, gaillardia, hollyhocks, pink and white bleeding hearts, columbine, and miniature rose bushes.

During our years at Coral Road, she never set out a single flower. Room was not a problem—we lived on two acres. The soil was good. But the uncertainty of our situation suppressed any desire on her part to arrange for her usual kaleidoscope of color.

In addition to my feelings of humiliation, I was also scared. I kept having that weak-in-the-knees sensation when you are facing a disaster where the limits are beyond imagining. I knew that if one of the banks foreclosed, their action would trigger a domino effect. It was a constant struggle to keep fear from turning into panic.

We did not know from one day to the next just what the Bank or the County was going to do. Fear feeds on tension and delay. If the County decided to lower the boom and file a tax lien, it would take precedence over any other financial encumbrance. Their action would virtually insure that we could not find any alternate financing.

My nerves became so raw, it seemed that every time the phone rang, I practically jumped out of my chair. We had a long gravel lane coming up to the Old House. I soon developed my own sonar system. I recognized the audible signature of each friendly vehicle by the sound their tires made when crunching the gravel.

Every time I heard a "gravel sound" I could not place, I died a little. I began to wonder, "Is this the end?" Will our adversaries take every penny we have and force the Center to close? One morning I heard a noise I could not identify. A wave of fear swept over me. How relieved I was to peek out my window from behind the curtain and see that our meter reader from the utility company had a different truck.

For the first time in my life, I began having nightmares on a regular basis. I realized from my reading that dreams only last a few seconds. It seemed to me, however, that I was being tormented for hours. Sometimes I heard imaginary voices whispering in the dark.

Some of my troubled sleep began to follow a familiar pattern. I had lost my way in a deep, dark forest. I kept running back and forth, trying to find a way out. Sometimes a rabid animal with a ferocious look was chasing me. I could have been drawing on my subconscious from the time that Lois was bitten by a raccoon with rabies.

In another night terror, I crawled under a building and became wedged. The more I struggled to get free, the more tightly I was imprisoned. I heard voices from somewhere and I cried out for help. No one answered. My sense of panic was unbearable. When I finally awakened, I was kicking and flailing the covers. Most of them were already on the floor in a tangled heap.

Many times, I went downstairs to fix a glass of warm milk and take several calcium tablets. I had been told that this procedure would help me get back to sleep. The milk and calcium usually worked; sometimes they did not help—my adrenalin was pumping so hard, all sleep had fled. I could either lie awake in bed the rest of the night or get up and go to work.

I have always enjoyed working. By the time I was in the fifth grade, I was earning all my own clothes and spending money. I received seventy-five cents a day working in the muck fields of Indiana. The work was hot and grueling. We crawled on our hands and knees ten hours a day weeding onions.

When I began preaching, I liked the ministry with all of its facets. I enjoyed the pulpit, teaching Bible School, visiting the sick and the lost, and so on. Because I was excited about my work, my energy level usually ran high.

But now, I was in a discouraging, foot-slogging situation where numbing fatigue became a constant companion. Just getting through each day was a victory. I had a daily struggle with depression. Sometimes my mind said to me, "Why don't you just throw in the towel and call it quits? Why put yourself through such misery?"

The officials from N-Bank kept sending us four or five page documents requesting detailed reports. By the time we responded to one questionnaire, another arrived. Many of these inquiries came from high-priced attorneys who were being paid several hundred dollars a letter for harassing us. The more they pursued us, the higher the amount they could bill the Bank.

We were engaged in a struggle on an uneven playing field. Although the officials can ignore *your* letters (and often do) the arrangement is not reciprocal. They hold the big end of the stick. You disregard their communications at your own peril.

Throughout the whole ordeal, I tried to maintain some kind of emotional equilibrium. If I broke under the pressure, I knew that the Center would probably go under. I felt I had to show a firm face to the outside world even though I was quaking inside.

We had staff members who knew our situation fully. They could not be demoralized by the faltering courage of the one who was leading them. My personal secretary, Joan B., was a jewel. She opened all the mail and read the letters that were sympathetic and kind as well as some that "raked us over the coals." She never wavered in her loyalty.

I could lean on those in other states who supported us, but geographically, they were too far removed from the war to assist in a battle strategy. Their prayers and encouragement, however, meant everything.

Because chief executive officers often have to make solo decisions based on their own sagacity and instincts, one hears the expression "lonely at the top." I can tell you from personal experience that it can also be "lonely at the bottom."

5. The Call At Midnight

I have already mentioned that in the midst of our struggles over Coral Road, the Center received a Matching Grant to do research on ministers in the Christian Church. The purpose of this study was twofold: (1) Find out how many ministers are leaving the preaching ministry; and (2) Launch a program to help hurting and discouraged ministers.

Any student who has attempted a study related to Christian Churches knows how difficult it can be to get accurate information. The leaders in our Brotherhood have never been much for statistics. They would much rather make history than record it.

After a year of research, we concluded that nearly half of the ministers in Christian Churches were dropping out of the preaching ministry. Even more alarming, a strong percentage of the remaining fifty percent were giving serious thought to leaving the pulpit. In checking with the leaders of other religious bodies, we found that our situation was similar to what they were experiencing.

In order to help stem the tide of ministers who were leaving the located ministry, the leaders of the Center launched a new program called "Safety Net." The name is taken from the high-wire acts in the circus where the performers know that if they make a misstep, the net below will help save them from plunging to their death.

Until a nationwide network of counselors could be established, most of the work fell on a handful of leaders in the Center. Early on, we often found that a heartening word at the right time could make the difference between a preacher's giving up or hanging on.

In addition to the development and publication of evangelistic resources, the National Church Growth Research Center has always been involved in Special Projects. I have spoken briefly of the American Festival of Evangelism, Congress 88, and the Washington Roundtable on Evangelism. I did not mention the Bicentennial Venture in Evangelism and the Washington Writer's Conference. The directors of the Center felt strongly that a Special Project to help keep preachers preaching was well within the purview of our overall aim.

When we first announced the program, we picked up the usual type of criticism that always accompanies a new enterprise. Eric Hoffer, the longshoreman philosopher, wrote a book demonstrating how adverse people are to change. One man reacted by saying that he knew of ministers "who were not fit to preach" and should be out of the pulpit anyway. I wrote back and agreed with him up to a point, but then I quoted my father who often said, "You don't shoot all the dogs just because some of them have fleas." But for the most part, the response from our Partners and the Brotherhood was highly favorable.

Many of the calls we receive from preachers in trouble are truly heartbreaking. The story has become a familiar one. The chairperson for the "church board" calls the minister aside after Sunday morning services and says they are having a "little meeting" that night. He wants the preacher to be there.

When the unsuspecting minister walks into the meeting, he finds that it is actually an ambush. A spokesperson for the group begins to read a long list of grievances against him. Some of the complaints may involve his failure to have called on a sick member of the congregation two years before.

One individual in the meeting is even shameless enough to read a list of criticisms from an anonymous letter. It has always been my position that if people are too cowardly to sign their name, their libelous letter has only one destination—the trashcan. But as the saying goes, "Any stick is good enough to beat a dog."

As the uncomfortable evening wears on, the preacher is stunned. He thought that his ministry was going along fairly well. Even though he knows that some in the congregation are lukewarm toward him, he has always been aware that "you can't make everyone happy all the time." Perhaps he is too inexperienced to recognize the telltale signs of serious opposition.

When he goes home from the meeting that night and tells his wife what happened, she begins to cry. Suddenly their whole world comes crashing down around them. They are both in shock.

During our years at Coral Road, I handled most of the Safety Net calls myself. We had not yet developed our group of nationwide counselors. I learned in seminary that effective counseling involves a willingness to listen. And so, I listened. Many times the calls came late at night and continued past midnight. I never hurried a minister off the phone, even if the call ran for two hours or more.

The caller often conveyed a collage of emotions—anger, pain, frustration, anxiety, hurt, and so on. He had been ordered to remove his books from the church office by noon the next day and to be out of the parsonage in sixty days.

As we investigated the matter further, we wanted to know what egregious sin or error the preacher had committed to deserve such treatment. As it turned out, he had simply made the kind of mistakes that every leader makes. But none of these slipups, it seemed to us, were serious enough for him to get "the axe."

While the distraught voice on the other end of the telephone was telling me that he could be out on the street in sixty days, I did not tell him, "If the Banks and the County have their way, I will be out on the street in thirty days."

What affected me the most during one of these anguished interviews was hearing the muffled sobs of the preacher's wife in the background. I have always been susceptible to a woman's tears, and listening to her cry was about more than I could take. Most of the time we were talking, I was having difficulty trying to hold back my own tears.

Lois and I found that our emotions were closer to the surface than at any other time during our married life. I have never been a "weeping prophet" in the pulpit (although I have not doubted the sincerity of those who cry while they preach).

I do remember the old saw about the custodian who discovered the preacher's sermon notes that he had absent-mindedly left on the pulpit. The janitor was startled when he read underlined in red, "Weak point; cry here."

During our worship service on Sundays, Lois and I found ourselves choking back the tears. Sometimes I could barely make it through to the end of my sermon. I often thought that I would have to sit down and let my message go unfinished.

The song service was even worse. As we sang the great hymns of the Church that have comforted and sustained the saints for centuries, I often had to quit singing. I could begin "Abide with me: fast falls the eventide;" but by the time I reached "When other helpers fail, and comforts flee," my voice grew husky and I was done.

We wept over the sympathetic notes and letters we received, especially from those we knew were struggling financially themselves. All gifts have meaning, but like that poor widow in the Gospels, we knew that some people were giving their mission dollars to the Center out of meager resources. Their gifts took on special meaning.

We felt a strong sense of obligation to be faithful and true to our mission and to garner every dime for Kingdom growth. We had an even greater incentive to keep rich Bankers and Bureaucrats from getting even richer by eating the lunches of poor people.

6. The Art of Worldly Wisdom

Of all the parables of Jesus, none is more difficult to understand than the parable of the Unjust Steward (Luke 16:1-9). A casual reading of the account seems to indicate that Jesus is commending dishonesty.

As the story unfolds, a steward finds out that he is about to be sacked. What is he to do? To guard against the future when he will be unemployed, he summons his master's creditors. One by one, he works out a strategy to lower their indebtedness. His motive is clear. He wants to have some friends who are obligated to him after his master gives him "the boot."

A more careful reading of the parable indicates that his master is not praising him for his under-the-table methods. He is congratulating him on his ingenuity in turning a difficult situation to his own advantage. The moral of the story: "The sons of this world are more shrewd in dealing with their own generation than the children of light" (Luke 16:8).

When Lois and I first moved to Washington, it was difficult for us to adjust to a blatantly predatory society. We had grown up under much different circumstances. Our fathers were both preachers in the American heartland. They served rural and small-town churches during most of their years in the pulpit. Between them, they gave the church over a century of preaching.

What we remembered from our childhood was the spirit of trust that pervaded the community. We never locked the doors to our home. If we had a key, we kept it under the doormat to the front entrance. Everybody knew it was there.

You left your car or truck unlocked from the day you drove it home from the dealership. You separated your car keys and left one in the ignition and the other in the lock to the trunk (Southern folks say "boot"). Consequently, you did not have to juggle two sacks of groceries in the rain and try to fish out your car keys at the same time.

The most frequent way of "signing a contract" was with a handshake. I watched farmers sell corn, beans, hay, and even a parcel of land with a firm clasp of hands. If the price of commodities increased dramatically over the next few weeks, the deal remained the same. If someone came along and offered a higher price per acre for their land, the deal still remained the same. It seems to me that the handshake deal of my boyhood was far more binding than the voluminous contracts of today.

It would be wrong to indicate that I was a stranger to the wiles and dangers of the city. Our family lived in inner city neighborhoods in Charleston, West Virginia, and Akron, Ohio. The school I attended in Chicago for postgraduate work was located on the west side in one of the most crime-ridden areas in the city. But to say that these experiences prepared me for the avarice of the Washington Business Community would be misleading.

Thomas Jefferson teamed up with the Baptists to promote religious liberty in Virginia. Although their theology was miles apart, Jefferson was thoroughly convinced that the only antidote for the poison of runaway capitalism was Christian values. Otherwise, rampant greed would cause the entire social structure to topple. As Robert Dick Wilson of Harvard observed years ago, "When the number of people who cheat exceeds the number who are being cheated, society collapses."

Power and money are the two aphrodisiacs of Washington society. Frequently, they are lodged in the same person. Washington business people, for the most part, are hard-driving, take-no-prisoners types. If your bad fortune turns out to be their lucky day—no problem! That is the way the game is played. Buying cheap and selling dear is the *summum bonum* of life.

If you put a group of avaricious business people on the board of a corporation, you have created some kind of monster. Someone has said that it is not the "crime in the streets" but the "crime in the suites" that is strangling America.

Greed is heartless. It has a hard face. It drains out the last drop of the milk of human kindness. Strangely enough, Adam Smith insisted that altruism is founded upon feelings of sympathy as innate as egoism; but in his *Wealth of Nations*, he based his economic theory on the universality of self-love.

104

The Old Testament prophets lash out against the rich "grinding the face of the poor." Isaiah asks, "What do you mean by crushing my people . . . says the Lord God of Hosts" (3:15). The prophet complains bitterly "each devours his neighbor's flesh" (10:20). He calls the corrupt leaders of his day, "greedy dogs" (56:11 AV).

Micah preaches, "They covet fields, and seize them; they oppress a man and his house" (2:2). Amos continues the denunciation of the greedy:

> Hear this, you who trample on the needy,
>   and bring the poor of the land to an end,
> saying, "When will the new moon be over . . .
>   that we may buy the poor for silver
> and the needy for a pair of sandals . . ." (8:4f)

In the New Testament, Paul tells Timothy that church leaders are not to be "greedy of filthy lucre" (2 Tim. 3:3 AV). The word "lucre" in the Greek means "silver." In other words, if you have an "inordinate or insatiable longing for wealth," then you are not fit to be a servant in the Kingdom of God. Only when you have tempered your passion through prayer and generosity can you be useful for God's purposes. Money becomes "filthy" when it is the object of covetous desire.

When you are dealing daily with those who are constantly trying to gain the upper hand, it is important to remember the parable of the Unjust Steward. Learn to benefit from the cunning behavior of those who want their own success even at the cost of your ruin.

Ministers tend to be talkative. After all, that is the way we make our living. But being too garrulous in a predatory business situation may cost you dearly. Here is a case where you learn that every phrase, and sometimes each word may count against you.

After several bad encounters, you learn to hold your cards just as close to the vest as your opponent (if I may be allowed a gambling expression). You express yourself on a strictly need-to-know basis. You tell the other person exactly what you want him to know—and no more. Even when you are not working in a tight business situation, it has been pointed out that most preachers get themselves in trouble not from their words in the pulpit, but from their conversations in the foyer.

Accuracy is always important, but especially in a legal situation. Make certain that what you say is true, or at least as correct as your information allows at the moment. Most real estate descriptions of a property for sale carry the following disclaimer: "Information believed to be accurate but should not be relied upon without verification." By using this method, agents can offer a property and at the same time protect themselves from the charge of misrepresentation.

One of the cynical expressions making the rounds of secular society says, "Nice guys finish last." Your temptation may be to become like those who oppress you. You can whisper to yourself, "If money is the name of the game, then I will get as much as I can. Then I will have the means to fight back." A dark side of you may say, "If I have to deal with barracudas, then I will become a shark."

The secret, it seems to me, is to learn from the world but not become like it. Paul exhorts believers, "Do not be conformed to this world but be transformed by the renewal of your mind, that you may prove what is the will of God, what is good and acceptable and perfect" (Rom. 12:2). In other words, until death comes, we cannot escape living in society; but we do not need to imitate the pagan culture that surrounds us.

Meanwhile, compassion and mercy need to be extended even to those who are enslaved by greediness. Covetousness has a way of sneaking up on us, just like alcohol, gambling, sex, or any other addiction. You can feel sorry for people who have made money their god because they have chosen so badly. When death comes, their riches will float out of reach like the tarpaper shacks along a swollen riverbank.

In our long struggle with Banks, we did have some high points of humor. When the officials of N-Bank summoned us for a "showdown" meeting, we were supposed to come with our tails between our legs. Andrew and I attended the conference along with an architect in our church who had gone head-to-head with zoning committees all over the Washington metropolitan area. We also included a member from the Executive Committee of the local NAACP.

As the conversation opened, Andrew pleaded with the bank officials not to call our loan. He reminded them that we had kept up our mortgage payments. He also said that in view of our other financial responsibilities, the timing was terrible. The officials refused to relent. Andrew's pleas for understanding were going nowhere. They said we had to pay up in thirty days.

Andrew said, "Well, if we can't pay and we have to have our church services outside in the rain, while we hold up our umbrellas, we will also display placards which read, 'Be sure to get *your* mortgage from N-Bank.'" Then he said, "We'll get a photographer and take out a full-page ad in *The Washington Post*."

For a moment, the tension broke. The four of us representing the Center cracked up. We began laughing so hard we could hardly stop. The two bank officials sat there like stones. Henry Adams wrote, "One must not try and amuse money lenders or investors." Thirty days passed and we did not hear a peep from N-Bank.

V.

Epilogue

The only people who did not
know they were beaten were the
English people themselves.

Becker

It is better to try brave things
and fail than to live in the twilight
of neither victory nor defeat.

T. Roosevelt

V. Epilogue

After the fall of France in World War II, the German High Command set their sights on the invasion of Great Britain. The battle plan was christened "Operation Sea Lion." In order to accomplish their objective, the British Royal Air Force had to be destroyed and the coastal defenses "softened up." The Luftwaffe was assigned the task of preparing for the landing craft. With their overwhelming air superiority, the German military leaders were supremely confident. It would take two weeks to destroy the R.A.F., a month at the most, they boasted.

With 3500 aircraft (historians vary in their estimates) which included bombers, dive bombers and fighters at their disposal, an around the clock attack on the English airfields and other military targets began. Later on, these air raids included the city of London itself. For 87 consecutive nights, an average of 200 bombers flew over dropping their deadly cargo. One of the most famous pictures to emerge from the war shows the dome of St. Paul's Cathedral silhouetted against the bursting flames of a burning city.

During the day, Londoners worked at their homes and factories. At night, they slept in the labyrinthine tunnels of their famous subway system called the "Tube." Each morning as they emerged, they witnessed the carnage of more air raids. When I was in London in 1950 to speak for the International Christian Endeavour Convention, I saw the damage from the bombings first hand. Much of the city was still in rubble.

Then one bright day, Londoners came up from the Tube listening for the deafening roar of the airplane engines and looking for the contrails in the sky. Instead, they were greeted only by the usual sounds of city life. All the enemy aircraft had gone. The Battle of Britain was over. The attack by the Luftwaffe had been blunted by a handful of courageous pilots and radar operatives.

In looking back on our own situation, it seemed for a while that we would be fighting Banks and Bureaucracy for the rest of our lives. We could hardly afford ourselves the luxury of thinking that our financial woes would someday subside. We knew, of course, that the Center could never be on easy street. No mission ever achieves such a secure status since the demands of world evangelization are endless. But now, at least, our enemies no longer held a club over our heads.

After the settlement papers for the sale of Coral Road were finally signed, Lois and I went back to the Old House. We were too weary to celebrate. The next day, I went downstairs to my study as usual. The weather was overcast. I sat in my chair looking out at the five magnificent oaks in our front yard, "a brotherhood of venerable trees" as Wordsworth put it. I loved those trees. I tried to work but I was too wiped out. I felt horribly flat. Then, I went back to bed—for two weeks!

From my reading, I learned that a fighter pilot was often so bone-weary following a mission, he had to be lifted out of the cockpit and carried to the barracks. In our circumstances, I did not know the full extent of my exhaustion. Propped up by adrenalin as we went from crisis to crisis, I could never allow myself to relax completely.

I had tried several vacations on the Outer Banks of North Carolina. I thought that the undulating ocean, the gorgeous sunsets over the Pamlico Sound, and the starlit nights could help soothe my jangled nerves. I do not remember staying the full length of time for any of these getaways. Some impending disaster always called me home.

The Spanish have a proverb, "Sooner or later, the hush comes to every home." Everyone has troubles—they just differ in kind. Lois and I feel that having experienced the harrowing time at Coral Road, we want to expand our efforts to help others in need. Etched in our hearts will always be the names of those who responded to our cries and came to our rescue.

One night at Coral Road in early spring, we heard the calls of our old friends. The geese were flying high overhead, headed north. Lois and I both rushed outdoors. The geese were winging their way back to the lush feeding grounds of the Chesapeake Bay and other wetland areas. Once again, they would find a nesting place and raise their young.

We watched until they flew out of sight. The old feelings of melancholy swept over us, but this time, instead of fear and longing, we had relief and rejoicing. But we also knew that Coral Road had left a mark on us that would remain forever. Like those Londoners who suffered through the German blitz, we would never be the same.

Benefactors

Meet the Vogels

Benjamin and Virginia Carol Vogel are Directors of Audio Resources for the National Church Growth Research Center and the Safety Net program.

Because of their generosity, thousands of audio-tapes have been sent to ministers and missionaries around the globe.

Benjamin E. Vogel was born March 22, 1940, in Iroquois County, Illinois, the son of Elmer and Mary Vogel. He graduated from Lincoln Christian College, Class of 1964, with majors in Ministerial Science and Christian Education. He earned the Master in Social Work degree from St. Louis University, St. Louis, MO, in June 1972. He recently retired from the State of Illinois after working almost 37 years as a Licensed Social Worker, practicing in the field of Mental Retardation. In 1961, he married Virginia Carol Arnett at the First Church of Christ, Catlin, Illinois. In 2001, they celebrated their 40th Wedding Anniversary.

Virginia Carol Vogel was born July 31, 1941, at Danville, Illinois, the daughter of Sidney and Bertha Arnett. She attended Lincoln Christian College for two years. Carol recently retired from a 25-year career as a Licensed Practical Nurse at the Christian Village, Lincoln, Illinois.

Ben and Carol are the parents of two children: Kenneth E. who died at the age of almost 28 years as a victim of cancer and Kristine E. (Nathan) Dolbeare who graduated from Lincoln Christian College with Bachelor's Degree in Sacred Music. She has served for more than ten years as a church administrator at Eastview Christian Church, Bloomington, Illinois. Mrs. Dolbeare received her Masters in Business Administration from Illinois State University on December 14, 2002. Her husband, Nathan Dolbeare is also a graduate of Lincoln Christian College.

Ben began recording sermons at Lincoln Christian Church, Lincoln, Illinois in 1972. This activity grew into what is now known as the Lincoln Area Tape Ministry. He purchased his first Professional Cassette Duplicating Machine in 1974. Ben and Carol have traveled thousands of miles over the past 30 years, recording various events and making the tapes immediately for sale to the participants of that event. Most of these events are religious or church meetings. Some conferences each year are in the area of Foster Care and Preventing Child Abuse.

In December 1990, Ben recorded the proceedings in the first meeting of a program that has come to be known as *The Safety Net*. This meeting was held at Westside Christian Church, Springfield, Illinois. In 1993, the first Annual Safety Net Conference was held in St. Louis, Missouri, just prior to the North American Christian Convention. The messages for each conference are available in a separate album.

Ben is also the editor of Paul Benjamin's sermon series albums, *Treasury of the Bible*. Each album contains 24 messages.